D1572314

PRIORITIES

Unless otherwise stated Scripture taken from the NEW AMERICAN STANDARD BIBLE®, Copyright © 1960, 1962, 1963, 1968, 1971, 1972, 1975, 1977, 1995 by the Lockman Foundation. Used by permission.

All enquiries regarding this publication and Peter McHugh's speaking engagements should be directed to:

Stairway Church
171 Rooks Road, Vermont, Vic
PO Box 3092, Nunawading BC, Vic 3131

Telephone: 61 3 9837 2900

Email: peter.mchugh@stairway.org.au

Printed and bound by Hyde Park Press, Richmond, South Australia

Book design by Philip Hopkins

ISBN: 978-0-9580771-4-9

PRIORITIES

DISCIPLE MAKING IN THE 21ST CENTURY

WHAT PEOPLE ARE SAYING

'I really enjoyed *Priorities*. It's easy to see the heart and passion of my good friend, Peter McHugh, on these pages. It has been a pleasure to witness Peter's own transformation from a good but intense servant to a joyful, loving son who has passion, power and authority. The book reflects his own journey.

'This book connects us to the primary purpose of God… 'let us make man in our image.' As leaders, whenever we put servanthood before sonship we are leading the church away from first love. Above all things our mentoring of people must lead them into a state of being God conscious, celebrants in this life.

'In this place of intimate connection we are empowered to take part in a process of discovering what is Kingdom normality and learning how to lay aside the religious substitute. Passive 'churchianity' is giving way to passionate spirituality. It's wonderful!

'Identity is the key to transformation. When we know God's identity for us, then we can receive and maintain the upgrade of who we are in Him. One of my favorite verses from the Message Bible is: 'God rewrote the text of my life, when I opened the book of my heart to His eyes.' 2 Samuel 22:25

'That is what Peter is doing here. He is authoring a re-write of the text of our life.'

Graham Cooke
Author, speaker, publisher
Santa Barbara, California USA

'I count it a privilege to call Peter McHugh my friend. It has been a joy to observe his spiritual journey over the years and to see how God has worked so deeply in his heart and life. I greatly admire Peter's humility, authenticity, vulnerability and courage to change and grow. What is currently occurring within his life and church community is nothing short of amazing. His latest book on discipleship is a timely call back to our God-given mandate, full of inspirational and practical insights. I highly recommend it!'

Mark Conner
CityLife Church
Melbourne, Australia

'In the last century, there has been so much emphasis in the church on becoming Christ-like, which of course, is the ultimate goal of discipleship. The problem is that we've redefined who Jesus is and how He ministered. We seem to have lost sight of the fact that the Person we are called to emulate was a counterculture revolutionary who walked in supernatural power. He lived, died, and rose again to deliver an ailing planet from the power of the devil and to extend the Superior Kingdom into every corner of the planet.

'In this powerful book, Peter McHugh unearths the real meaning of the normal Christian life and teaches us how to walk in our divine mandate as world changers and history makers. *Priorities - Disciple Making in the 21st Century* is a clarion call to all Believers to raise up powerful, supernatural wonder-working Jesus people and to make disciples of all nations.

'It's very possible that Peter McHugh's book could equip you and your disciples to fulfill your divine destiny. Whether you're a high-maintenance, low-impact believer living a boring Christian life, or you are a mature leader looking for tools to empower your followers, this book is for you!'

Kris Vallotton
Senior Associate Leader, Bethel Church
Redding, California USA

'As the church in the Western world finds itself increasingly at odds with the community it is seeking to touch for Christ, there are lights being lit by the Holy Spirit that deserve our attention. Peter McHugh and Stairway Church are on a journey. God is moving in Peter's life; the testimony of Stairway Church deserves to be heard and the message of *Priorities* deserves to be digested by every leader who longs to see Christ lifted up in our broken world. Read it, and see if you don't find your heart crying out for the life it testifies to. It's time for change.'

Allan Meyer
Co-founder, Careforce Lifekeys International
Melbourne, Australia

'Peter McHugh has painted a canvas that sharply juxtaposes the life of the average believer in the 21st century with the radical lifestyle of true 1st century discipleship. In an honest and biographical account of his own journey and that of his spiritual community, Peter leads us through numerous stories into a profound revelation about the nature of true discipleship. We are called to bring heaven to earth and to walk as Jesus walked!

'The thing I love about Peter's warm and attractive writing style is the way he draws us into his own heart journey in a manner that inspires and invites us to walk with him. Peter is a great leader because he is committed to being a great follower! This book finally gets the sequence right; our new lifestyle flows out of the discovery of our new life in Christ. We are sons on a journey out of the old orphan heart who are destined to manifest the glory of sonship. The old paradigm of discipleship focused on performance and outward conformity. The new paradigm recovered from Scripture focuses upon new creation realities that lead us to manifest true freedom and great power. I highly recommend this book that will inspire you on the path of becoming a disciple who releases the glory of the Father everywhere you go.'

Phil Mason
Spiritual Director, New Earth Tribe
Byron Bay, Australia

'This is a powerful progression from Peter McHugh's three previous books. For some time now there has been a deep ache in my heart about discipleship paradigms within Australia (and probably the Western world generally). This book addresses the key issues which I sense will give new life and power to Christian discipleship and therefore Christian Community (church) and Mission.'

Keith Farmer
Former Principal of the Australian College of Ministries
Spiritual Mentor for many Australian Christian leaders
NSW, Australia

'Discipleship has been and is at the forefront of God's heart. I believe that God is emphasising this in the church in this hour, right now. In *Priorities – Disciple Making in the 21st Century*, Peter McHugh takes us on a journey with a community of believers whose passion is to be like Jesus. With candor, vulnerability, and authenticity, Peter explores the issue of what true disciple making is. It's not about what you do but who you are. It's about looking like Jesus. Backed by incredible testimonies of the fruit from their church, he calls us to experience the freedom of what God has to offer us as sons and daughters. This concept is very counter-culture in the church today but one I am grateful Peter is trumpeting.

'As always, Peter points us back to an encounter with God and living in His presence. This book is not only revelatory but also refreshing in its approach to discipleship. What Peter and Stairway Church have discovered in sustaining a culture that creates true disciples is critical for all believers. I recommend anyone who wants to grow as a son or daughter of God to read this book.'

Banning Liebscher
Jesus Culture Director
Bethel Church
Redding, California USA

'Peter McHugh has written a book filled with truth, God stories, personal experience, and amazing revelation. *Priorities - Disciple Making in the 21st Century* is a must read for every church leader and disciple maker. There is no doubt in my mind that this book is a tool that the Holy Spirit is using to prepare leaders to disciple nations and build a glorious church on the earth. As you read the pages of this book you are sure to be empowered and encouraged in your personal walk and in your ministry. I am honoured to say that Peter has not only written a brilliant book, but the truths you are about to read are being lived out in his life and in his ministry. I can honestly say that I believe that this is quite possibly one of the most important books written for the 21st century church!'

David Wagner
Father's Heart Ministries
Pensacola, Florida USA

'Every once in a while a book comes along that you just know is going to have a powerful and far reaching impact. This is one of those books! Today many in the church world are talking about the desperate need to change but are often not sure why or how. Peter gives us simple insights and effective tools to bring about healthy and fulfilling change. Peter's calm style and conviction of truth is birthed from a sequence of divine encounters. His love for the presence of God is profound and has shaped in him an integrity and humility of heart. Furthermore the credibility of this book is not just in academic theory but is in the authentic, observable journey that Stairway Church is adventurously advancing in. We salute you Stairway and thank you Peter. This book is for any believer in Church who is eager to see Heaven fill earth!'

Rob Rufus
Founder and Lead Pastor of City Church International
Hong Kong

'Few people I know are as qualified to write a book on making disciples in the 21st century church as Peter McHugh. His foresight and wisdom to transition a community of faith (a sizable one) that was predominantly 'church focused' into a community that is now 'Kingdom focused' has been remarkable to watch.

'The church is in the middle of one of the greatest reformations ever; many in the future will talk and indeed write books about what is currently under way. Wherever you find yourself in your own personal journey this book will help you 'join the dots' as Peter takes you on a journey within his own community, as he and others transition people to be disciples of the Kingdom, equipping them to truly bring heaven to earth.

'There are many testimonies included in the book of ordinary everyday folk now living extraordinary lives as they have come to understand who they are 'in Christ'. I highly recommend this book, knowing it will have a radical impact not only in your life but in others that you have influence over.'

Gary Grant
Friends First Church
Melbourne, Australia

'The journey Peter takes us on in his latest book *Priorities,* doesn't leave us with a list of 'to do's', but compels us to establish a legacy of love, life and light in the community we find ourselves in. We discover by making the main thing, the main thing, we inherently create an empowering space for Father to be Father, and us, His children, to be all he has made us to be and do. Life will take a radical simplicity when we embrace a life of kingdom priorities.'

Gary Morgan
Hillview Community Church
Melbourne, Australia

"What should a disciple of Jesus look like and how are they made?'

'These are critical questions for the church. In *Priorities,* I believe Peter McHugh captures the voice of the Spirit and helps answer the cry of those dissatisfied with out-dated and ineffective notions and practices of disciple-making. What makes *Priorities* particularly valuable is that it provides a window into the ways in which Peter and Stairway Church are putting this new paradigm of disciple and disciple-making into practice.'

Murray Averill
Senior Pastor, Nexus Church
Queensland, Australia

'Peter McHugh's book, *Priorities – Disciple Making in the 21st Century*, reverberates with the sound of exploration and process. Peter articulates brilliantly well the journey of discovery, query, revelation and understanding, as he and Stairway Church endeavour to answer the question *'If we are making disciples, what would a "completed one" look like'?* That question sounds easy enough on the surface, but meaningful answers beg for a deeper dig, considering that most quick answers can be trite, and can mitigate empowered kingdom solutions. Traditional mindsets, and therefore the solutions derived from those mindsets, perpetuate many of the discipleship problems that have dogged the church for centuries. The cry is for a workable and replicable model of discipleship that is freeing, fruitful, empowering and more easily sustained.

'One cannot read Peter McHugh's book without recognising the well-defined challenge to average-and-agreed-upon discipleship mindsets. Those mindsets deserve to be disturbed, deconstructed and perhaps discarded. Having suitably disturbed the reader, Peter sets about with sensitivity, intelligence, stories and examples, to purposefully influence the reader into an engagement with transformation and transition. That the church needs to embark on transition is a given. How to make that journey and translate it into effective disciple-making is the heart-journey of this book. You are invited, even urged for the sake of the Kingdom, to take that journey! Don't be surprised that you find yourself heart-captured on the way through.'

David Crabtree
Senior Leader, DaySpring Church
Castle Hill, NSW, Australia

'In the book *Priorities*, Peter McHugh paints an amazing picture of what the church should look like, cultivating the presence while making the supernatural relevant in our everyday walk with Jesus. I personally have had the honor of pouring into Stairway Church and have witnessed the fruit of a community that continues to take risks into uncharted territories, bringing Heaven to Earth in their city. In this book you will discover that you were born to be part of a generation of revivalists who are called to co-labour with heaven's core values and priorities. If you have a hunger for God and have a desire for Him to become manifest in your life then I would highly recommend this book.'

Chad Dedmon
Bethel Church
Co-Author **The Risk Factor**
Encountering Jesus Ministries
Redding, California, USA

'In *Priorities*, Peter McHugh presents a book of testimonies as much as anything else; hundreds of real life stories that reposition what the 'normal Christian life' looks like. It is full of people's stories of stepping out in faith, trusting that God is leading them by the Holy Spirit to engage Him in their day-to-day lives. 'Success' is all about having a go rather than in the outcomes, even though some of the outcomes are absolutely remarkable. This book will shake some up significantly. If there is anything that today's followers of Jesus need to develop it is a sensitivity to the Holy Spirit through a yielded life. This book gives a peek into a community of faith that is stepping out in a way that most would dare to dream of. Read it if you dare.'

Dale Stephenson
Senior Pastor, Crossway Baptist Church
Melbourne, Australia

'I have been refreshed by Peter's other books immensely – particularly the level of openness and vulnerability in which he writes. This book however, stands out from the rest in that it strongly urges us the reader to self-examine and re-evaluate what makes us believe the things we believe AND hence do the things we do. In this book, Peter displays an uncanny and humble ability to really involve us,by gently, but unashamedly calling us to be Berean in our approach to what we are believing and therefore doing. He does this by clearly mapping a journey that has been taken by an entire community of people – no mean feat in my estimation! To underestimate the power of the process and transformation would be a mistake no leader or individual would ever wish to make! It is not only a "must read", it is unquestionably a "must think " – it certainly has scratched where I itch!'

Rob Buckingham
Senior Minister, C3 Bayside Church
Melbourne, Australia

'Iranaeus of Lyons, an early church father said, 'The glory of God is the human person fully alive.' Being a disciple of Jesus has always been about living the God life now, embracing the glory of our *imago dei* and engaging with the redemptive work of heaven's influence all around us. In this book Peter helps us to re-imagine how the interplay of heaven and earth affect and implicate us in the story of God.'

Greg Burson
Edge Kingsland
Auckland, New Zealand

CONTENTS

ACKNOWLEDGEMENTS

One of the many wonders of life is walking with a group of splendid friends, colleagues and associates. A book like this is ultimately a team effort. My team have been outstanding and I want to publicly acknowledge their invaluable contribution.

To all from Stairway and beyond who have told their stories to illustrate and bring my text to life, I remain inspired by you and grateful for your courage.

To Paula Taylor, my hard working, diligent and 'can do' personal assistant (and friend). We both know that without you this project would still be a handwritten manuscript.

To Allan Meyer, Gary Grant and Gary Morgan who faithfully read, dissected and improved my best effort at a draft. Your gracious and insightful comments are now viewed as my insights!

To the editor, Liz Kemp. Your editing expertise and commentary have made this book much more readable and accessible than I would have been capable of producing on my own.

To the book designer and longtime member of Stairway, Phil Hopkins. Your layout and eye for creative detail makes it a pleasure to handle and view my content.

To Graham Cooke, Keith Farmer, Kris Vallotton, Murray Averill, Mark Conner, Rob Rufus, Banning Liebscher, Phil Mason, Allan Meyer, Rob Buckingham, David Crabtree, Dale Stephenson, Chad Dedmon, Gary Grant, Gary Morgan, Greg Burson and David Wagner. Your endorsements are kind, encouraging and true!

DEDICATED TO

Stairway church, who have been absolutely brilliant as together we have walked off our map into a brave new supernatural world.

And to,

My beautiful wife Lyn; awesome children, Hannah, Erin and David; their spouses David, John and Christy; and my heart-stopping grandchildren, Josiah, Mikayla, Jack and Aiden – your love and support mean everything to me.

FOREWORD

A significant part of my life is spent travelling to the nations of the world to serve their leaders. I'm not sure if I know anyone as intentional in their pursuit of God and His purposes as is Peter McHugh. Every year I share my heart to the people in Stairway Church. The next year I observe how they've applied themselves to that word and have done so with diligence, integrity, and excellence. The fruit is remarkable. The transformation that has taken place within the church is starting to spill out into society. That was their goal, and they have done it well.

I must admit I approached this book with an extreme bias, having watched Peter and his people travel on this amazing spiritual journey for close to a decade. Because I have already seen the fruit of the materials in the book, I expected it to be great. And I wasn't disappointed.

I love it when profound things are practical. It's a sign of great maturity when someone can take great truths and break them down into bite-sized pieces. What you'll find in *Priorities: Disciple Making in the 21st Century* are truths that have been lived out in the trenches of everyday life. Today many leaders look to Peter as a model, a coach, and for some, a father in the faith. It is a beautiful thing to behold. Thankfully, we now have a book that helps break down this leader's approach to making disciples in response to the commission of our Master.

Priorities: Disciple Making in the 21st Century was born in the context of community – a group of people who have said a resounding yes to the transformational purposes of God. It wouldn't be a bad book if it were theories and concepts, as truth is truth. But these principles have been tried in the fires of relationships and proven in the context of a church's transformational pursuit of the King and His Kingdom. In other words, this book is real. And their city is reaping the blessings as a result.

We start our walk with Christ with the deep realisation that we sinners are in need of a saviour. Tragically, many fail to move past that concept of themselves once they are forgiven. As a result, they strive to obtain what God has already given them for free – worthiness through Jesus Christ. The author lays again a foundation for believers to truly shed their incorrect self-image and discover the identity that was given to them the day of their salvation.

This book also offers tools for transitioning from that place of confinement into a place of freedom and empowerment. Learning to partner with what has already been available is only attained through our identity, recognised in our love relationship with the Father. This identity comes when we no longer perceive our heavenly Father as a judge. That moves us into a culture of freedom as we realise we are not required to perform, but to abide in Jesus and become grounded in the expectation of direct access to God. This creates a community of people in pursuit of becoming like Jesus and surrendered to the Holy Spirit in His mission to touch the earth.

My greatest encouragement in reading this book is in the testimonies sprinkled throughout. When I first started speaking at Stairway Church, I would bring them the God stories from my life to encourage them and help them consider what God wanted to do in their city. My testimonies are now unnecessary as they have an absolute deluge of stories from their own experience. This is a people that have grabbed hold of this mission, believing that nothing is impossible.

What they have done to steward and press in for the miraculous and take extreme risk at Stairway Church, is the most encouraging and inspiring manifestation of the Kingdom being hungrily taken hold of and demonstrated through willing people. Peter has beautifully pastored his people by hungering and taking risks himself. His impact comes from his eagerness to learn the ways of the Father, and anyone who knows this man's heart is without excuse. I recommend this book to all those who desire to do the same.

Bill Johnson - Senior Pastor of Bethel Church in Redding, CA
Author of *Hosting the Presence* and *When Heaven Invades Earth*

PREFACE

In His unbounded love, God became what we are, that He might make us what He is.

– Saint Irenaeus –

One of the aims of *Priorities - Disciple Making in the 21st Century Church* is to draw the reader into considering that an effective disciple who makes an impact on their community and reproduces themself will be:

- Beholding and becoming like Jesus, not performing and striving to do things for Jesus;
- Living in the knowledge that comes from experiencing the Spirit of adoption, not living under the burden of an orphan spirit that tries to be something they already have;
- Conscious of their Sonship and how heaven can invade earth through them, not conscious of their sin, questioning whether they are worthy to be used for God's purpose;
- Primarily focussed on intimacy with God and being aware of His presence, recognising that a lack of intimacy leads to a performance-based spirituality and religion;
- Living out of what they have already received because of the work of the cross, **not** trying through their own effort to get what is already theirs;
- Committed to seeing that all of life is spiritual and every circumstance offers the opportunity to examine the beliefs in their heart;
- Managing what they believe **above** managing their behaviour, and;
- Recognising that their principle responsibility is identity **not** destiny.

This book rests on the foundations and shoulders of my first three books.

You and the Creative Power of Frustration explores the idea that frustration can be a friend and not an enemy. Our frustration tells us that we have reached a limit in our emotional, social, psychological, spiritual and/or physical capacity. It defines for us an opportunity to grow in our capacity. We can discover how to employ our frustration much as a servant who points out a reality with potential to change. Frustration does not reveal what is impossible to achieve or become. A healthier outlook is to see it as a gift that can mark the acquisition of personal insight into the possibility of change. Then we can engage in a change process to move into a bigger and brighter future.

A Voyage of Mercy is a very personal and revealing exploration of how I was led to address the areas of my own frustration. As a husband, father, friend and leader I was frustrated with my, at times, harsh response to others. When I was under pressure I was not treating others with love and respect. I was aware of a need to be in control that had the consequence of leaving others feeling hurt, marginalized and uncertain. My leadership would take on a drivenness that reached for power and control to achieve my desired outcomes. These were not the trademark responses of love and compassion of Jesus.

As I allowed these frustrations to become my instructors, I discovered places of fear. I was able to identify a fear of failure, fear of rejection, fear of being misunderstood and fear of being taken advantage of. When I was under pressure, these unconscious fears would begin to influence my behaviour. Behaviour is always an echo of belief. Therefore, behaviour is changed when our beliefs change. I began to realize that my fear (**False Expectations Appearing Real**) was generating belief patterns that resulted in the manifestation of behaviour I was unimpressed with. The bible says that perfect love casts out all fear. As I was leading with my fear it revealed that I did not know deeply enough the love God had for me.

A Voyage of Mercy chronicles the process that the Lord led me through to receive the knowledge of His love for me. To illustrate the process, I drew on very personal email communications from that time, including reflections from my staff that provide an insight to the changes they observed and experienced. The net result was that the encounter I had with God's love for me dealt a deathblow to my fear - and my behaviour has been changing ever since.

Above the Line - Reshaping Relationships and Communities in the 21st Century looks to how individual Christians and faith communities balance being known by their fruit (John 15: 8) with being known by their love (John 13: 35). Where a national and/or ethnic culture primarily defines a person's identity, value and significance based on their performance, the result is that people are 'working for' acceptance. Experiences of love are often based in and conditional upon appropriate behaviour and results. Value and significance are often unconsciously defined by performance. The net result is that most national and ethnic cultures are orientated towards 'fruitfulness' as the foundation for expressing and experiencing love.

The thesis of *Above the Line* proposes that the majority of churches and their leaders have unintentionally carried the performance bias of their particular culture into how church culture is formed and expressed. Diagram One visually represents this thesis.

A MODEL TO REFLECT UPON

UNITY OF **HEART**	AFFECTION	PRESENCE	WINE	KNOWN BY **LOVE**
UNITY OF **PURPOSE**	ACHIEVEMENT	PRINCIPLES	WINESKIN	KNOWN BY **FRUIT**

DIAGRAM 1: THE ELEMENTS THAT SHAPE CULTURE

In *Above the Line* the place of being known by our fruit in church life focuses on:

Achievement – how many members; how many salvations; how many baptisms; how much money, how many churches planted; how many small groups; etc.

Principles – how to lead; how to be a disciple; how to be successful; how to parent; etc.

Wineskin – the way church meetings are conducted; the hymns/choruses sung; what ministries are formed and expressed; what is appropriate preaching; etc.

These are all important and significant matters. They must be considered and designed with consistency and integrity. Matters of stewardship require accountability, responsibility and clarity in these areas. However, how much attention should they be given in the light of the biblical priority of love? (Matthew 22:36–40; 1 Corinthians 13)

In *Above the Line* the idea of love, in church life, focuses on:

Affection – this is a narrow description of love, however, it is a 'concrete' idea in that it is possible to assess how much affection an individual feels towards God, self and others.

Presence – speaks of our desire for God, our pursuit of God, our reliance on God and our commitment to God.

Wine – Is a metaphor for the place of God's activity in our hearts and in our midst corporately; it is the place of celebration, fellowship, friendship and fun.

These three are designed to be benchmarks to help the reader consider how love is being expressed in a church or community of faith.

Above the Line proposes that the performance bias of a culture so strongly influences the focus of churches and Christians that 70 – 80% of their time, energy and life together is based on 'below the line' activities. The highest Christian value is love, however it only receives 20 – 30% of our attention. If this is true - and it was for myself and the church I led - how can we change so that we focus 70 – 80% of our lives on 'above the line' matters, without losing sight of the significance and importance of 'below the line' characteristics? For example, we are to plan by principles but live by presence. All churches (and individual Christians) need to function with both love and fruitfulness in mind. A church's culture will be determined by which of these two functions is allowed to dominate.

Above the Line explores how the church I lead had started the process of change towards living primarily 'above the line'. This quietly revolutionary book begins with the premise that the change process is built on encounters with the love of God. These encounters shape and form our belief and our behaviour.

The principles articulated in *You and the Creative Power of Frustration* were applied to my own life in the context of my fear. The result was an encounter with God's love that is chronicled in *A Voyage of Mercy*. As a consequence love began to be expressed far more profoundly in every area of my life. However, as I changed I realised the culture of the church I led needed to also be shaped and formed by love. *Above the Line* describes how and what we focussed on to begin this cultural transformation of the church and its members.

Priorities – Disciple Making in the 21st Century focuses on how our cultural transformation has influenced the way we make disciples. Jesus' departing words to His followers before ascending to heaven were:

> But the eleven disciples proceeded to Galilee, to the mountain which Jesus had designated. When they saw Him, they worshipped Him; but some were doubtful. And Jesus came up and spoke to them, saying, "All authority has been given to Me in heaven and on earth. Go therefore and make disciples of all the nations, baptizing them in the name of the Father and the Son and the Holy Spirit, teaching them to observe all that I commanded you; and lo, I am with you always, even to the end of the age." (Matthew 28:16–20)

> Afterward He appeared to the eleven themselves as they were reclining at the table; and He reproached them for their unbelief and hardness of heart, because they had not believed those who had seen Him after He had risen. And He said to them, "Go into all the world and preach the gospel to all creation. He who has believed and has been baptized shall be saved; but he who has disbelieved shall be condemned. These signs will accompany those who have believed: in My name they will cast out demons, they will speak with new tongues; they will pick up serpents, and if they drink any deadly poison, it will not hurt them; they will lay hands on the sick, and they will recover." So then, when the Lord Jesus had spoken to them, He was received up into heaven and sat down at the right hand of God. And they went out and preached everywhere, while the Lord worked with them, and confirmed the word by the signs that followed. (Mark 16:14–20)

Churches and their leaders know they are called to make disciples. However, I wonder if it is time to articulate what a disciple should look like from God's perspective? This is the story of our adventure in becoming disciples of Jesus – disciples whose priority is to release heaven on earth. What started as my personal voyage was taken up by our core leadership and has since become the triumph of the people of Stairway Church. Who we have become and how we express that identity has been made possible because those within our community of faith have encouraged one another to believe we can all invade the impossible. This book is **our** story.

My aim for Priorities is to draw you into our journey through the use of numerous testimonies. You will encounter the intentionality that followed from our re-discovery that we are all mandated by heaven to be like Jesus. It is my prayer that you, the reader, will be exposed to encounters with God that will impact your theology and nourish your desire to be a complete disciple of Jesus.

Chapter One
TO BE LIKE JESUS

If I'd asked customers what they wanted, they would have told me, 'A faster horse!' People don't know what they want until you show it to them.

– Henry Ford –

MEGA OR META CHURCH?

The Lord is awakening His people all around the earth to embrace a fresh understanding of how He sees the normal Christian life. To embrace this awakening He will clearly not contradict His word... however, He is comfortable contradicting our understanding of it!

As a congregation at Stairway we have come to see that we are disciples through whom Jesus wants to invade earth. He taught us to pray: 'thy kingdom come, thy will be done on earth as it is in heaven.' That is, on earth *as it is in* heaven. Prayer is always accelerated through our immediate action.

Prior to embracing this reality in 2007 we were focussing on programmes, systems and methodologies to make better disciples who attended church regularly, were part of a small group, who tithed, who had been baptised in water and the Spirit, and who lived with good character and morals. Our focus was on people *coming* to church over and above *becoming* the church. We were making disciples from a focus on 'below the line' characteristics of achievement, principles and our wineskin. We were on our way to becoming what the literature refers to as a 'mega church'.

Colin Dye[1] on Facebook, June 13, 2011 writes:

The rise of the Western Mega church phenomenon in the 1980's was championed by church growth proponents who seemed to believe that the objective was to grow a single church into a huge congregation of many thousands. The primary purpose was to attract and keep as many people as possible under one roof. The preaching had to be popular and the programme polished. 'Big' became the new spirituality and 'better' the new philosophy of ministry. The small group programme was simply a way of 'closing the back door' of the church.

Where all these elements successfully came together, usually under the leadership of a talented and anointed leader, the multitudes came. Some were new converts but most were drawn from other churches within a hundred mile radius. This couldn't be further away from what David Yonggi Cho, for example, was doing in South Korea. He also had a church of many thousands and excellence was highly valued. However, ***discipleship was at the centre of the strategy.*** People were not passive spectators in Sunday services but active members who did the work of Christ through the cells and brought their 'fruit' to the massive celebrations in the church building at the weekend. This is not Mega church, but Meta church.

Meta church is about reaching many thousands, but it is also about building church through Jesus' method of discipleship. What is the point of attracting thousands of believers into a massive building once a week, if there is no real, intentional discipleship? *Meta church seeks to train and deploy every member for the harvest,* and not just to attract them into one central venue. It is about releasing people into the ministry through a network of cells, congregations and celebration gatherings resulting in a multiplicity of interrelated expressions of Christ throughout a city or region.

THE POWER OF MINDSETS

Mindsets are extremely powerful. They shape our expectations, values and behaviour. For example, the Israelites anticipated a messiah who would bring vengeance and defeat to their natural enemies. Jesus anticipated that, as the Messiah, He would bring vengeance and defeat to the enemy of all mankind, that is, Satan. Consequently, the Israelites failed to recognise the Messiah because of incorrect mindsets that had shaped their expectations.

It is true that God will never contradict His word. However, it is equally true that He does not mind challenging our understanding of it. This is well illustrated by the occasions where Jesus healed on the Sabbath, much to the disgust of the Pharisees. Luke 13:14 says:

But the synagogue official, indignant because Jesus had healed on the Sabbath, began saying to the crowd in response, 'There are six days in which work should be done; so come during them and get healed, and not on the Sabbath day.'

The official missed so much because of his theology based purely on the law. How many other healings had he seen in his lifetime? Why was he unable to rejoice and celebrate with the woman whose life had been totally changed? What stopped him from seeing that Jesus was ushering in a time of grace where God would be revealed as a Father again? When Jesus contradicts our understanding of His word, how do we respond?

We have challenged our mindsets about being a community of faith by asking the questions:

- What is the normal Christian life?
- If we are making disciples, what would a 'completed' one look like?

The journey so far has brought staggering outcomes, many of which I hope to reveal through the pages of this book.

As I begin, it would be good for us to ponder and celebrate just two of these stories.

The nose that could not smell...

'I was at the hairdresser and I was told by the owner that she could not smell smells.

I felt God prompt me to pray for her healing – that she should be able to smell all the lovely smells there were to be smelled.

I offered to pray for her and she said yes, although she said she did not believe in any of this sort of thing.

I stood in the front of the shop, it was winter so it was dark outside and I was the last in the shop so all the other hairdressers all lined up to watch what I was doing and so I felt very self conscious (highlighted in the bright shop window with people passing by, about ten hairdressers all lined up to watch, praying for someone who did not believe it would work, but who was willing to let me pray for her – I felt intimidated by her, her attitude and the people).

I placed my hand on her and prayed for healing – I prayed that she would smell the fragrances of Heaven and that she would be totally well.

I felt nothing; no anointing, nothing. She said she felt nothing at all as well.

I was so embarrassed, but I kept it light and went home that night and cried in the kitchen and said to A that it was all too hard and that I just wanted to give up – taking the steps of faith was hard and I couldn't do it anymore.

A said that he felt that it was just a step for her in her walk towards God – which encouraged me somewhat, but I still felt lousy and angry at God for 'making a fool of me'.

I felt responsible that she felt nothing and that nothing had happened and I felt like an idiot knowing that I had to go back there for haircuts in the future.

I shrugged it off, kept stepping out to pray for people and kept going to the same hairdresser for my haircuts – even so I felt ashamed and hoped I would not see her again and I did not mention the night to my usual hairdresser.

Well, about six months later – I had resolved to keep pressing in and praying for others – the girl I had prayed for saw me and said she had been wanting to see me for ages... she said for the last six months she had been smelling things that she had never smelled before, and that she kept telling my particular hairdresser 'can you smell that, I can smell that, I could not smell that before, I can smell things I could not smell before'.

I was so glad I had kept going, and here the encouragement was six months after the event. I learnt that I am not responsible for the outcome and that whether they feel the anointing, or I feel the anointing, while nice and reassuring is not necessary - God moves as he chooses.'

Miracles definitely happen...

'Thought I would update you guys on the friend I told you about who was having major problems with her pregnancy...

Just to remind you of the background to this:

After having a shocking run of complications last year, my friend fell pregnant in December with twins and was very excited. One day soon after she fell pregnant, we bumped into each other and I felt strongly to ask her if it was ok for me to pray for her for a great pregnancy. She agreed, but since she is not a Christian, was a little cool about it.

Last month, I bumped into her again and she looked absolutely shocking. She told me that she had just come back from her doctor's and was being encouraged to terminate the pregnancy due to one of the babies being profoundly disabled and both babies appearing to have severe heart defects. She was in a shocking place and very conflicted, as you can imagine. She told me that some Christian family members had said to her that her babies were damaged due to her 'sinful' lifestyle and that she needed to repent. Obviously she was angry and confused and very sad.

I just sat with her and cried with her, one: because I didn't know what to say or do, and two: because I recognised that her situation was horrible and an impossibly hard one to find herself in. I asked her again if she minded if I prayed and whether she would mind if I got some of my friends to pray for her and her family. She said yes and I prayed, explaining that God was crying with us and that He felt her pain and just wanted to hold her during this tough time. I told her that He was a God of miracles and that He cared for her and her babies dearly.

The next day, I got some of the young adults in our YA connect group to agree to fast and pray with me, as well as some friends of mine. Within six days, she rang me to say that the nuchal fold measurement which was showing severe Downs Syndrome in numerous previous tests had now REDUCED from a 6.8 reading to a 3.5 reading, which was approaching a normal reading. She said that neither she nor her doctor could understand this change at this stage of the pregnancy, but that it was a great sign and that instead of terminating, the doctor had suggested she wait another 3 weeks for further tests and decide after that. She begged me to keep praying (how cool!).

Well, yesterday was the end of the three weeks and I got a very excited phone call from the doctor's office. Both babies are looking fine, the nuchal fold reading is normal, the blood tests are normal, there is no fluid in the brain or stomach of either baby and the heart defects appear to be totally gone!

In her words: 'Miracles Definitely Happen!'

As a nurse and healthcare professional, it was so much easier for me to go to a place of 'realistic expectation' and just be resigned to this 'sucky' situation, but I'm learning to go to a place of expecting that my Papa God has a better idea and REALLY WANTS to make a 'sucky' situation into a brilliant encounter with His love.

I'm really overwhelmed at how amazing He is - this 'crossing the chicken line thing' is definitely the place we are meant to live from! Yay Papa!'

You will discover many more stories at godtestimonies.wordpress.com

WHAT DOES A DISCIPLE LOOK LIKE?

As followers of Jesus, our mindsets are established by our theological persuasion. At the risk of oversimplifying this point, I want to suggest that the big theological question that has shaped church life and matters of discipleship has changed in the last twenty-five years. When Martin Luther sparked the Reformation, the big question he was addressing was: *What must I do after I am saved to continue on to heaven?* His understanding of justification by faith resulted in a need to challenge how the church was adding practices to guarantee entry to heaven.

Over the last twenty-five years a new big question has emerged: *What must I believe to see heaven invade earth through me?* The way each question is answered has a significant impact on how we view the normal Christian life. It follows, then, that the way in which we view the normal Christian life determines what a disciple looks like and how we make disciples.

In order to create context for the following chapters I offer this summary of what disciples can look like under the influence of these two questions.

WHAT MUST I DO AFTER I AM SAVED TO CONTINUE ON TO HEAVEN?	WHAT MUST I BELIEVE TO SEE HEAVEN INVADE EARTH THROUGH ME?
Disciples get to heaven by growing in character and doing what church people do: • Go to church regularly; • Tithe; • Attend a small group; • Service in church programmes; • Go to prayer meetings; and • Pursue spiritual disciplines.	**Disciples** release heaven on earth by: • Recognising God's presence in everyday life; • Pursuing friendship and intimacy with God as a son; and • Focussing on releasing His reign on earth daily.
Faith is a belief system that primarily affects where someone lives in the afterlife.	**Faith** is about spirituality and impartation of the Kingdom in the here and now.
Servants who work for the Lord.	**Sons** who work with the Lord.
Identity is based on what you do – performance.	**Identity** is based on who you are – acceptance.
Manage behaviour and focussed on my destiny.	**Manage** belief and focussed on my identity.
Soul driven, as I once was by my fear.	**Spirit** led as a mark of sonship.
Discipline is a change of behaviour in an attempt to be holy.	**Discipline** is a change of attitude to align with being like Jesus.
Focus on 'below the line' activities.	**Focus** on 'above the line' activities.

DIAGRAM 2

A good friend of mine, Allan Meyer shared the following words, which I think are particularly helpful:

'I'm reminded of a student at least twenty years ago after an intensive elective on Galatians who summed it up memorably: *Almost no evangelical church would ever say you are saved by works, but once you 'get in' by grace through faith, then it becomes all works-oriented. It's like a ritzy country club wanting to grow its clientele, so they offer a one-year free trial membership. But after that, if you want to stay in, you pay through the nose!* That seems to be what the first column is getting at, with the second column as the refreshing alternative.'

Our awakening at Stairway into a new understanding of what the normal Christian life looks like and, as a consequence, the manner in which we make disciples, was stimulated by considering our beliefs about what it really means 'to be like Jesus'.

For those whom He foreknew, He also predestined to become conformed to the image of His Son, so that He would be the firstborn among many brethren. (Romans 8:29)

We are to be conformed to His image. This brings a focus on the following:

- what I know of the Father's love for me;
- how I love others through forgiveness; not judging; blessing those who curse me; compassion;
- to Whom my life leads people;
- how I recognise and work with His presence to heal, to deliver, for miracles, signs and wonders, and;
- living as a much-loved son.

This focus is underpinned by the observation that the primary theme of the gospel of the Kingdom is God's love and response to people, *not* the sinful nature and condition of people. The gospel of the Kingdom as preached by Jesus emphasised how God receives sinners with love, mercy and kindness and *not* a focus on correcting what is wrong. Jesus didn't come to make bad people good, He came to make natural people supernatural.

The father in the story of Luke 15:11-32 received his lost son on the basis of his sonship, not his worthiness. Being worthy was the son's focus. The focus of the father was 'you were born my son and will always be my son – allow me to restore you to that position'. The rulebook of the Old Testament that focussed on sin has been replaced by the grace of the cross that acknowledges restoration of sonship through faith. We enter relationship with the Father as sinners saved by grace (Ephesians 2:8) but continue the journey into being sons because of the work of the Spirit (Galatians 4:5-7).

God is love, so His affection for and belief in me is based on *who He is* not *what I do*. To that end, trying to be worthy to be a son is illegitimate as it diminishes the finished work of the cross. This is why John writes in his gospel (John 1:12): *'But as many as received Him, to them He gave the right to become children of God, even to those who believe in His name'*. Our **identity** should cause us to live as children of God; that is, Jesus was the firstborn and we are thus able to be like Him in every way. Then John writes in his first letter (1 John 2:6): *'the one who says he abides in Him ought himself to walk in the same manner as He walked.'* Here the word 'abides', comes from the Greek word *meno*, which means 'to remain in' or 'to stay alive in'. This speaks of friendship with God if you are a guy and **intimacy** with

God if you are a girl! Therefore, through our intimacy (friendship) with God we get to be like Him – in every way.

Out of our identity in and intimacy (friendship) with God John now writes in his gospel (John 17:18): *'As You sent Me into the world, I also have sent them into the world.'* Just as the Father sent Jesus to **influence** the world, Jesus has sent us.

We continue to influence the world in the knowledge of what John wrote in his gospel (John 14:12): *'Truly, truly, I say to you, he who believes in Me, the works that I do, he will do also; and greater works than these he will do; because I go to the Father.'*

Our **inheritance** is to do what Jesus did... and greater. We should at least begin with what Jesus did first. So once again we get to be like Him in every way. Rivers of living water flowing out towards others and their circumstances. (John 7:37-38)

What if our understanding of being a disciple has been influenced by ideas of getting to heaven rather than releasing heaven on earth?

What if our idea of what it is to be a disciple and what a normal Christian life looks like has been corrupted by our culture and its bias towards an identity based on performance?

What if there is much more to the normal Christian life than we had previously imagined?

DISCIPLES MANAGE THEIR BELIEFS

And do not be conformed to this world, but be transformed by the renewing of your mind, so that you may prove what the will of God is, that which is good and acceptable and perfect. (Romans 12:2)

As we at Stairway were awakened to the possibility of needing to review our theology around the matters of identity, intimacy, influence and inheritance we observed that Paul began the majority of his letters with matters of believing. Matters of behaviour would then follow. We are discovering that if we mentor people's behaviour (for example, improving their prayer life), when they don't experience significant change they feel like a failure, lose confidence and believe they lack worth. However, if we focus on people's beliefs (for example, 'God is totally committed to having a relationship with you without reference to your sin'), their behaviour of seeking out a prayer life is transformed. Paul understood this truth that right believing leads to right living. Put another way, behaviour is always the echo of belief. Take for example, anger. Nobody *makes* us get angry. We *choose* to get angry. Although some people are very good at creating the environment where the choice to be angry is easier for us to make (behaviour) because we believe something.

Paul also recognised that what we believe is strongly influenced by what we have experienced of God; how we have encountered Him. For example in Ephesians 3:19 he writes: 'and to know the love of Christ which surpasses knowledge, that you may be filled up to all the fullness of God.' The original Greek renders this scripture as: 'to know *by experience* the love of Christ...', in other words, experiential knowledge surpasses what we intellectually learn – 'head knowledge'. It does not replace it; rather it *is*, so that we may be filled to the fullness of God. This same Greek word is used in John 8:32: 'and you will **know** (in an experiential way) the truth, and the truth will set you free.' It is also used in John 17:3: *'This is eternal life, that they may know (in an experiential way), the only true God, and Jesus Christ whom you have sent.'* So, in our journey of transformation into being disciples and understanding the normal

Christian life from God's perspective, we need to not just learn about God but position ourselves to experience Him.

Church leaders have significant influence in shaping beliefs about 'what makes a disciple of Jesus?' and ' how does God define the normal Christian life?' With this in mind we/they need to be clear that our/their definitions are a reflection of Kingdom life and not simply church life and/or the leader's vision. We have concluded that making disciples is the privilege of helping people to be like Jesus in every way, wherever they are. We are releasing empowered sons of God to fulfil their God-given assignments. All of life is spiritual and provides daily opportunities for heaven to invade earth through us.

It is also important that, when making disciples, church leaders remember that New Testament disciples have the privilege of being internally governed through a relationship with the Spirit and the word. This is what John is pointing to when he writes:

As for you, the anointing which you received from Him abides in you, and you have no need for anyone to teach you; but as His anointing teaches you about all things, and is true and is not a lie, and just as it has taught you, you abide in Him. (1 John 2:27)

In the Old Testament, followers of YAWEH were externally governed by the law (Deuteronomy 30:15-20) and disciples motivated by blessing and avoiding punishment as they were told what to do and controlled by expectation. In the New Testament, disciples are to be motivated by love and relationship as they are Spirit led to do what is right.

In order to follow this line of reasoning to its natural conclusion. church leaders should endeavour to make disciples by ruling with the heart of a servant and serving with the heart of a king. When they rule with a servant's heart they use their favour to empower others to step into their destinies. People become free to dream around leaders like this. Leaders who serve with the heart of a king do so knowing that they have access to everything needed to meet their needs, that is, the unlimited resources of the King.

As I conclude this chapter I want to offer some thoughts on the process of mind transformation in the context of discovering what the normal Christian life is. We have found that the transformation process can actually be described as deconstruction. Deconstruction is a consequence of choosing to be like Jesus; it is not to oppose something. It is an outcome of pursuing kingdom culture and values. It is the beginning point, not the ultimate purpose.

Deconstruction is based on hearing the Spirit's guidance as to what to embrace and then allowing that to grow to displace the old mind sets. It accepts paradox over paradigm. That is, the need to be a 'both/and' thinker, not 'either/or'. For example, disciples are both sons and servants; they need to be presence-orientated and purpose-driven; and it is necessary to have both above and below the line characteristics. (See my previous book *Above the Line – Reshaping Relationships and Communities in the 21st Century Church*.)

Deconstruction helps people upgrade from reconciliation to relationship with God. Because wine is a belief system, new wine is a re-shaped belief system. Therefore, we must build communities of faith who love the learning, who embrace process and can be flexible. Consequently they can embrace the idea that weakness can be a joyful vulnerability and also that if there is a negative there must be a positive.

Here are two more amazing stories that illustrate the disciples we are becoming and the Christian life we are experiencing.

Stepping out and taking a risk...

'... I was challenged at work to pray for a colleague... not just pray, but I felt God wanted me to lay hands on this woman and pray for her. Fairly easy if someone is receptive to God... not this woman... she is so far left she is almost toppling over and her view of God is that he is heartless and mean because he allows so much injustice, pain and hurt within the world. Needless to say, we have had some interesting conversations where at one point she actually said that God was evil...

'Hmmm...' I thought '... so, God, you want me to lay hands on her... okay'.

This lady had fallen over and not only shattered her left elbow but also dislocated it. She had to have surgery and the comment from the surgeon was that it was like putting together a puzzle there were so many pieces!

So, one day I was bold and asked if she would mind me praying for her, (as in privately in my bedroom, not actually with her...no great challenge there, nice and comfortable!) – to which she replied – 'that would be nice'.

God nudged me further – 'I want you to lay hands on her' to which I replied – 'you have to be kidding – you know how she feels and what she is like.' He said 'I want you to lay hands on her...'

'Okay' I said... 'but I am trusting you to do something here.'

So the next day early at work an opportunity arose and I boldly asked if I could lay hands on her elbow and pray for healing. Amazingly, she agreed and away I went, thinking, 'God, you'd better show up here'.

I prayed specifically that the pain would go (she was in a lot of pain at that time) and that her bones would knit together perfectly so that she would have full use of her arm again. Her next x-ray was on the 22nd December 2010 and I believed the elbow was going to be healed.

22nd December rolled around and she had her x-ray. The radiologist reported that there was still a big crack and the bone hadn't healed – she was devastated. I simply told her 'I'm still believing it will be healed completely and the first report is not the last'.

Finally she saw the Doctor who looked at the x-ray and said there was still a small crack – (not a big one as the radiologist had reported) and that she could take her sling off, which was giving her so much grief. She has a lot more use in her arm than she expected.

So while things are not back to 100%, I believe that seeds have been sown in her heart that God does care about her and will heal her completely.'

Healing in an 'ivory tower' of the law...

'I work at a large law firm in the city. I was in a small galley tea room making a cup of tea when one of the tea ladies, R, who cleans the kitchens and collects cups from offices etc. came in. We have known each other for many years. I asked how she was and she said she had been having terrible pain in her shoulder and neck for two or three weeks.

Without stopping to think, I asked if she would like me to pray for her. Her eyes almost popped out of her head. I explained I was a Christian and I believed God wants to, and does, heal people through prayer. She said 'I believe, I believe'. I got permission to place my hand lightly on her shoulder and neck. I could feel the muscles were like concrete. I asked the Spirit to come and waited, then prayed peace for R's body, mind and spirit and healing for the muscles and joints in her shoulder and neck. As I prayed I felt some movement in the muscles under my hand, the stiffness seemed to be going. After a while I asked her what was happening for her. She said 'Its fine, it's wonderful', moving her shoulder around and; 'your hand was so hot'. (I didn't feel any unusual heat in my hand but she did.) She said she had a small amount of pain in one part of her neck so we prayed again. Then a man came into the tea room and said 'What's this – reiki in the tea room?' I said, 'this isn't reiki – this is God'.

I saw R later that day in the same tea room with another tea lady. She had experienced complete healing from the pain. She thanked me and called me her doctor and I told her that I was very happy to pray for her but it was Dr Jesus who healed her. R was cool with this as she has an Eastern Orthodox background. Another tea lady, N, said she had terrible pain in her arm and a lump on her upper arm. I offered to pray but two other people wanted to come into the tea room (and there was no room) so she said another time. R keeps telling her story to most of the non-legal staff and still calls me and Jesus her doctors when she sees me.

A few days later N came by my office on her rounds and she said she didn't want to bother me, but I asked if she would like prayer. She let me feel the lump on her upper arm through her shirt and there was a raised lump the size of a 10 cent piece on her upper arm. We prayed in my office and the pain in her arm reduced a lot (but not completely) but the lump disappeared – neither of us could feel it.

When I asked her the next day how she was, she said the pain was reduced but a small lump had come back – it was much smaller than before and I could feel it was much smaller. So I prayed again and again the pain reduced. I told her I would pray for her anytime. I said if the lump persisted after we had prayed a few times she should consider seeing a doctor. She said she had more faith in God to heal than doctors.'

CHAPTER TWO
WHO AM I?

You have made us for Yourself and our hearts are restless until they rest in you.

– Augustine –

The normal Christian life is to be like Jesus, in every way. The problem we face is that we know we do not live like Jesus; therefore how can we possibly be like Him in every way? We are aware of our failings, our fears and doubts, our inadequacies, our sin and our inabilities. For example, we know we cannot heal the sick, so how can we be like Jesus in that way?

Hannah is a teenage girl in our congregation. I will let her tell you her story in her own words from the email she sent:

Faith and courage of the young...

This is what happened from the people I prayed for. The first person that I did was Maddy and she had left ankle problems and so we prayed for her and then she felt a warm and fuzzy feeling and she felt a little bit better.

What happened to Maddy was the same as what happened to another girl but with her back. There was this other lady who had about 6 or 7 out of 10 in terms of pain and when we prayed for her, her ankle felt about 3 or 4 and so we did it again and she ended up being like a 1 and so we prayed once more and she only had ¼ out of 10 in pain then. There was another lady who had a very bad problem with her ankle and she had the pain for about six to twelve years and the doctors had been trying to work out what's wrong and trying to make it better and so we prayed for her a couple of times and she didn't feel any pain. There were another two ladies who had been needing some encouragement but they haven't had much, mostly they had just had discouragement. We prayed for them and they felt really good and one of the girls wanted to give me a hug and I said yes they could.

There was this man who came up and he needed some encouragement too, because he had been sick and the doctors gave him some drugs to help him get better and he got addicted to them. He just needed some prayer so he could get off them and so we did and he felt God a lot and fell down, not like he fell down by accident. It was God.

It was a bit scary to pray for the first person but after a while I got the hang of it and I didn't know if they heard me or not, but I just kept praying.

THEN on Sunday night when Jen and Brian were at church singing, I was lying next to mum soaking. Mum told me that there had been feathers falling and I lay down and I was talking to God and listening to the music and I felt like I was in a cradle with God rocking me to help me go to sleep and I started to feel like I was the baby being rocked and I woke up and God picked me up and made me feel better. I also heard angels singing during worship and this other lady also said she heard angels as well.

While I was on the carpet I was praying for feathers and I didn't know it, but mum had also been praying for feathers for me. The next morning I woke up and found really, really, really fluffy white feathers on my rug like the ones that were falling at church! I know God gave me feathers because He can and to let us know that he is there and that He is real and listens to us when we are talking to him.

Hannah is disarmingly honest about how she sees herself in this situation. Yet she also recognises that her relationship with Jesus trumps how she views herself. Like many of us, Hannah is learning to discover truth of how to see herself and her relationship with God.

The emphasis on *'What must I do to be saved?'* has resulted on a focus on managing behaviour and therefore invariably a focus on sin. Many followers of Jesus are comfortable with indentifying themselves as *'sinners saved by grace.'* (Ephesians 2:8) It is absolutely true that we enter the Christian life through the doorway of 'sinners saved by grace'. However, it is the front door into a mansion of 'new things' that became ours when we were born again.

NEW THINGS HAVE COME

In 2 Corinthians 5:17 Paul writes:

Therefore if anyone is in Christ, he is a new creature; the old things passed away; behold, new things have come.

What are the new things that have come? What has changed so that we not only pray, 'thy kingdom come, they will be done on earth as it is in heaven' (Mark 6:10) but we actually live out this prayer by fulfilling Jesus' words in John 14:12: *"Truly, truly, I say to you, he who believes in Me, the works that I do, he will do also; and greater works than these he will do; because I go to the Father"* while also being bold enough, like Jesus, to declare to the world: *'if I do not do the works of My Father, do not believe Me'. (John 10:37)*

Nicodemus' conversation with Jesus helps us to grasp that the new things that have come are a consequence of being 'born from above', 'born in the Spirit' (John 3:1-8). We have certain characteristics and abilities because of our natural birth. Equally our spiritual birth has established characteristics and abilities to live with and for God. The Holy Spirit is at work in our lives so that we might know these things that have been freely given to us by God (1 Corinthians 2:12).

2 Peter 1:2-11 continues this theme in his second letter when he writes:

Grace and peace be multiplied to you in the knowledge of God and of Jesus our Lord; seeing that His divine power has granted to us everything pertaining to life and godliness, through the true knowledge of Him who called us by His own glory and excellence. For by these He has granted to us His precious and magnificent promises, so that by them you may become partakers of the divine nature, having escaped the corruption that is in the world by lust. Now for this very reason also, applying all diligence, in your faith supply moral excellence, and in your moral excellence, knowledge, and in your knowledge, self-control, and in your self-control, perseverance, and in your perseverance, godliness, and in your godliness, brotherly kindness, and in your brotherly kindness, love. For if these qualities are yours and are increasing, they render you neither useless nor unfruitful in the true knowledge of our Lord Jesus Christ. For he who lacks these qualities is blind or short-sighted, having forgotten his purification from his former sins. Therefore, brethren, be all the more diligent to make certain about His calling and choosing you; for as long as you practice these things, you will never stumble; for in this way the entrance into the eternal kingdom of our Lord and Saviour Jesus Christ will be abundantly supplied to you. (2 Peter 1:2–11)

Peter wants us to be diligent in being certain about 'His calling and choosing' us. He calls our attention to the fact that we have already received everything pertaining to life and godliness. He answers us that we can be partakers of the divine nature as we act out our faith and 'in this way the entrance into the eternal kingdom of our Lord and saviour will be abundantly supplied'.

The work of the cross provided so much more than the forgiveness of our sins. As important and foundational as this is, forgiveness of sins is just the beginning of the exciting adventure represented in Jesus' words: 'As You sent Me into the world, I also have sent them into the world' (John 17:1). We have been saved **from** sin but we have also been saved **into** a life of being like Jesus.

To give Jesus His full reward for all He attained for us at the cross we must accept that one of the most important 'new things' that has come is the identity we now have in Him as sons of God (Galatians 4:7). We are the righteousness of God in Christ Jesus (2 Corinthians 5:21) and as such we can walk on the earth in the same manner as He walked (Colossians 1:10).

Peter and John's response to the lame man at the gat Beautiful in Acts 3 powerfully illustrates that the disciples had grasped this reality. When they declared, 'look at us', they knew who they were and what they had to offer. This seemingly impossible situation had been created for them as sons of God. Just as Jesus declared in Luke 4 the prophetic certainty that He was anointed for the miraculous, Peter and John knew that this was now their truth and reality also. They were so confident about what they carried and who they now really were that even Peter's shadow healed the sick (Acts 5:12–16).

THE PLACE OF IDENTITY

Jesus made the will of heaven His priority. He showed us that the normal Christian life included heaven invading earth through us. To be this sort of disciple requires that we repent and believe in the gospel. That we yield and surrender the identity we have established in growing up in our humanity and cultural expectations to the identity we have in Christ. Our existing personal and cultural identity is shaped predominantly by experience and interpretation of what others say about us and do to us. It follows, then, that our new identity as a son of God (Galatians 3:26) is shaped predominantly by experiences and encounters with God. As previously stated, it is what we know by personal experience with God that sets us free beyond what we learn about God through study. Our experiences with God that are transformational and establish our identity as his son come through renewing the mind (Romans 12:2) and beholding God and becoming like Him. (2 Corinthians 3:18) Paul helps us grasp the significance of this transformation in the book of Romans.

Paul asserts his confidence in the gospel when he writes:

For I am not ashamed of the gospel, for it is the power of God for salvation to everyone who believes, to the Jew first and also to the Greek. For in it the righteousness of God is revealed from faith to faith; as it is written, 'but the righteous man shall live by faith.' (Romans 1:16–17)

In the context of Romans, Paul is at pains to make sure the reader is placing their confidence in the gospel of **grace** not the gospel of the **law** (works). He writes:

because by the works of the Law no flesh will be justified in His sight; for through the Law comes the knowledge of sin.

But now apart from the Law the righteousness of God has been manifested, being witnessed by the Law and the Prophets, even the righteousness of God through faith in Jesus Christ for all those who believe; for there is no distinction; for all have sinned and fall short of the glory of God, being justified as a gift by His grace through the redemption which is in Christ Jesus; (Romans 3: 20–24)

Paul is highlighting here some fundamental matters affecting our identity in Christ. That is, one of the many 'new things' that we have received by being born again. These fundamental matters are:

- Justification, that is, being the righteousness of God in Christ

Jesus, is a gift of grace because of the work of the cross and our faith (belief) in that work (verse 21).

- The works of the law (our behaviour) will not bring justification, that is, I am worthy in the sight of God because of Jesus' behaviour not my behaviour (verse 20).

- Importantly, Paul states that a focus on the law and works brings about consciousness of sin (verse 20). As Paul progresses through his conversation with the Romans this matter of sin consciousness grows in significance. He draws out in Romans 6:11 that we have to choose between sin consciousness and being conscious of God. 'Even so, consider yourselves to be dead to sin, but alive to God in Christ Jesus.'

For Paul, our consciousness of God results in living as sons of God:

If Christ is in you, though the body is dead because of sin, yet the spirit is alive because of righteousness. But if the Spirit of Him who raised Jesus from the dead dwells in you, He who raised Christ Jesus from the dead will also give life to your mortal bodies through His Spirit who dwells in you.

So then, brethren, we are under obligation, not to the flesh, to live according to the flesh — for if you are living according to the flesh, you must die; but if by the Spirit you are putting to death the deeds of the body, you will live. For all who are being led by the Spirit of God, these are sons of God. For you have not received a spirit of slavery leading to fear again, but you have received a spirit of adoption as sons by which we cry out, 'Abba! Father!'' The Spirit Himself testifies with our spirit that we are children of God, and if children, heirs also, heirs of God and fellow heirs with Christ, if indeed we suffer with Him so that we may also be glorified with Him. (Romans 8:10–17)

Paul is both conscious of his sin and conscious of his righteousness. Paul addresses the place, influence and power of his sin when he says. 'but if by the Spirit you are putting to death the deeds of the body , you will live.' By relying on the Spirit, being conscious of God, Paul identifies that those people are the sons of God and that from this position they address their sin.

A little earlier in his dialogue with the Romans, Paul has considered this issue of sin consciousness and how to deal with it. He begins in Chapter 7:

For we know that the Law is spiritual, but I am of flesh, sold into bondage to sin. For what I am doing, I do not understand; for I am not practicing what I would like to do, but I am doing the very thing I hate. But if I do the very thing I do not want to do, I agree with the Law, confessing that the Law is good. So now, no longer am I the one doing it, but sin which dwells in me. For I know that nothing good dwells in me, that is, in my flesh; for the willing is present in me, but the doing of the good is not. For the good that I want, I do not do, but I practice the very evil that I do not want. But if I am doing the very thing I do not want, I am no longer the one doing it, but sin which dwells in me.

I find then the principle that evil is present in me, the one who wants to do good. For I joyfully concur with the law of God in the inner man, but I see a different law in the members of my body, waging war against the law of my mind and making me a prisoner of the law of sin which is in my members. Wretched man that I am! Who will set me free from the body of this death? Thanks be to God through Jesus Christ our Lord! So then, on the one hand I myself with my mind am serving the law of God, but on the other, with my flesh the law of sin.

Chapter 8

Therefore there is now no condemnation for those who are in Christ Jesus. For the law of the Spirit of life in Christ Jesus has set you free from the law of sin and of death. (Romans 7:14–8:2)

Paul powerfully asserts that his response to his sin is not to live with condemnation (8:1). Paul responds to his sin by relying on the Spirit of life in Christ Jesus to set him free from the law of sin and death. That is, he focuses on being conscious of his new identity as a son and relies on that identity to shape and form his life as a follower of Jesus. As we stay focussed on our standing as sons of God we can be led by the Spirit.

As we live as sons of God we can be like Jesus because we begin to live as 'heirs of God and fellow heirs with Christ.' Being like Jesus is always undermined and stolen from us when we become sin conscious. That is, when we are defined by, focussed on ruled by and dictated to by our sense of being unworthy because of sin. When we are sin conscious we come again under a spirit of slavery leading to fear (Romans 8:15).

Yet it is absolutely important to recognise that our sin does not disqualify us from being sons of God. The story of the prodigal son in Luke 15 will help us at this point.

I will get up and go to my father, and will say to him, "Father,

I have sinned against heaven, and in your sight; I am no longer worthy to be called your son; make me as one of your hired men.'" So he got up and came to his father. But while he was still a long way off, his father saw him and felt compassion for him, and ran and embraced him and kissed him. And the son said to him, 'Father, I have sinned against heaven and in your sight; I am no longer worthy to be called your son.' But the father said to his slaves, 'Quickly bring out the best robe and put it on him, and put a ring on his hand and sandals on his feet; and bring the fattened calf, kill it, and let us eat and celebrate; for this son of mine was dead and has come to life again; he was lost and has been found.' And they began to celebrate.

"Now his older son was in the field, and when he came and approached the house, he heard music and dancing. And he summoned one of the servants and began inquiring what these things could be. And he said to him, 'Your brother has come, and your father has killed the fattened calf because he has received him back safe and sound.' But he became angry and was not willing to go in; and his father came out and began pleading with him. But he answered and said to his father, 'Look! For so many years I have been serving you and I have never neglected a command of yours; and yet you have never given me a young goat, so that I might celebrate with my friends; but when this son of yours came, who has devoured your wealth with prostitutes, you killed the fattened calf for him.' And he said to him, 'Son, you have always been with me, and all that is mine is yours. But we had to celebrate and rejoice, for this brother of yours was dead and has begun to live, and was lost and has been found.'" (Luke 15:11–32)

The prodigal son was sin conscious to the point of believing he was not worthy to be his father's son. Worthiness was not a consideration for his father; he was not focused on his younger son's sin but only on his sonship. The father sought to restore him to that position, refusing to count the son's transgressions against him (unlike his older brother). The younger son, in the father's eyes, was never disqualified by his sin from being his son. In just such a way God the Father does not negate, diminish or lessen our right to be sons of God (John 1:12) because of sin. The devil, through religion and a works-based faith, is determined to stop us living as sons of God by leading us to be sin conscious. We live as sons of God by relying on the spirit of adoption, the spirit of life in Christ Jesus and crying out 'Abba! Father' even though we do sin.

Sin consciousness is the most destructive force that stops God's people living the normal Christian life and being like Jesus in every way. Sin consciousness is unintentionally and inadvertently fuelled by the performance bias of our national and ethnic cultures. Christians carry this bias into their faith life and it is translated into works. 'What must I do to stay saved and go to heaven?' In some respects we are no better than our forefathers when we read:

I am amazed that you are so quickly deserting Him who called you by the grace of Christ, for a different gospel; which is really not another; only there are some who are disturbing you and want to distort the gospel of Christ. But even if we, or an angel from heaven, should preach to you a gospel contrary to what we have preached to you, he is to be accursed! As we have said before, so I say again now, if any man is preaching to you a gospel contrary to what you received, he is to be accursed! (Galatians 1:6–9)

You foolish Galatians, who has bewitched you, before whose eyes Jesus Christ was publicly portrayed as crucified? This is the only thing I want to find out from you: did you receive the Spirit by the works of the Law, or by hearing with faith? Are you so foolish? Having begun by the Spirit, are you now being perfected by the flesh? Did you suffer so many things in vain—if indeed it was in vain? So then, does He who provides you with the Spirit and works miracles among you, do it by the works of the Law, or by hearing with faith? (Galatians 3:1–5)

IDENTITY THEFT

In the book of Genesis the devil tempted Adam and Eve to become like God through their own effort, by eating the fruit, when they were already like God because they were made in His image. Religion can be defined as trying to establish through performance what we already have through grace. The devil tried to challenge Jesus' identity in the wilderness (Luke 4:1–13) and again played the performance card. Identity theft has always been high on the devil's agenda.

Sin consciousness is a significant contributing factor to the work of identity theft that the powers of darkness are bringing against God's people. It would seem that God knows who we are: sons of God. That the devil knows who we have already become: sons of God. The whole of creation is waiting eagerly for us to realise who we are: sons of God (Romans 8:19). It seems that we, the sons of God, are the only ones who don't know who we are!!

I wonder whether Luke 19:9–10 may provide some help in this area of identity theft: 'And Jesus said to him, "Today salvation has come to this house, because he, too, is a son of Abraham. For the

Son of Man has come to seek and to save that which was lost." It is important to note Jesus refers to 'that which is lost', not 'those who are lost'. With this in mind, Jesus aligns salvation with the matter of identity, being a son of Abraham. Is it possible that Jesus came to restore, through salvation, the identity of people as sons of God?

In Genesis 1:26 we read:

Then God said, 'Let Us make man in Our image, according to Our likeness; and let them rule over the fish of the sea and over the birds of the sky and over the cattle and over all the earth, and over every creeping thing that creeps on the earth.'

Skip Moen[2] provides some helpful insights into how to interpret or exegete this page with the word **image** in mind. One of the principles of exegesis is looking at the text as if we were part of its intended audience. In other words, we need to know what the words would have meant to the people who first heard them. Most believers, however, read the bible as if it were written to them in their present culture and context. So the Genesis account of the foundation of man was written for an audience recently removed from the polytheism of Egypt. Consequently our understanding of the language and its meaning must be discovered within the culture of the ancient near-East, not within the framework of our Greek-based empiricism.

Genesis was not written as science. It can be argued that Genesis was written as a deep myth, that is, a cultural explanation of the reason, purpose and origins of the world. (This doesn't mean it isn't true or it didn't happen.) The Genesis story of creation is arguably an explanation of **purpose** rather than an account of the mechanics of creation. When we read the first three chapters of

Genesis as an *explanation of purpose* it causes substantial shifts in our interpretation. None is more important than the shift in the meaning of the word for image - '*tselem*'.

A typical exegesis of the Genesis account begins with the presuppositions of our empirically based, scientific perspective, not from the worldview of the ancient near-east. Therefore, we treat a word like *tselem* (image) as if it describes attributes attached to an existing substance. We answer questions like '*What does it mean to be a son?*' with reference to physiological, psychological and spiritual attributes. This leads to the idea that God created some substance called 'man' and filled that substance with features associated with our idea of human being. But this isn't the way ancient near-Eastern mythology works.

Moen proposes that in context, Genesis 1:26 is answering the question, '*Why does God form man?*', and the answer is to 'rule'. In other words the emphasis of the text is not on the apparent attributes of human beings but rather on the purpose of *being* human. In ancient near-Eastern cultures men did not rule: they served. This is a significant difference between the Hebrew deep mythology and other explanations. In Hebrew thought, men are in partnership with God and are elevated to the place of ruling, a function that is the sole prerogative of the gods. In other words, the Hebrew explanation of the formation of Man is focussed **not** on Man's essential substance but rather on Man's assigned purpose.

Culture determines the meaning of a word. The word *tselem* would be recognised by the community at Sinai as a work describing an idol, a representation of a god. Coming out of Egypt, the community had ample experience of Egyptian idols. The crucial point is that the idol is **not** the god; it is merely an icon or representation of the god. Nevertheless, it retains all the power of the God so that in pagan thought it is appropriate to worship the idol as if it were the god. Of course, the God of Israel demonstrated in word and deed that all other gods represented by idols were in fact not gods at all. But the concept of **representation** still adheres to the word *tselem*. When the audience heard the story of God's formation of Man, there would have been an immediate connection between the power of God and the representation of that power in the image of God in Man. Man is therefore the 'idol' representation of God.

We must understand the 'image of God' as a description of the role and action of God (His power), not as a summary of enduring attributes, as the Greek view would suggest. A man is a man when he acts as the representative of God's power. To be in God's image is to act like God acts.

In Hebrew culture, what it means to be human is to act as the representative of the power of God. Perhaps our tendency to read the Genesis account as a universal description of the creation of all biological 'human' life is really the result of a paradigm; a paradigm that comes to us from the Greek idea of a common essence of humanity. Perhaps Genesis is a story about the origins and purposes of the tribe of Abraham, and only the tribe of Abraham – and we are invited to join that tribe and share in its story. With this in mind it is possible that we as human beings have been the victims of identity theft. Have we been robbed of our true purpose and been seduced by a Greek paradigm of what it means to be human when biblical evidence seems to suggests otherwise?

Here as some stories of people who are learning to live out of their new identity as a son of God and not be influenced by their earthly identity.

Three girls blessed...

Sarah

I was buying a cheese slicer at Southland, when I felt inclined to say to Sarah (the girl serving me) that she had a lovely gentle and kind spirit.

She responded that she did not feel that way and that her boys sure would not because she had yelled at them to hurry up to get ready for school that morning.

I said that her yelling at them did not change the fact that she had a gentle kind spirit. I then explained that I was a Christian and I believed that God spoke to me about people and that I felt He said that she had a gentle kind spirit. She said she felt like it was the nicest thing anyone had said to her.

I then asked her if she would like me to pray for her and she would feel that peace and God's peace in her. She said yes and asked if I was like those healers that lay hands on people – she has a girlfriend who does that. I wanted to correct her about 'healers' but decided instead to pray for her.

She said that she certainly felt something as I prayed for her and that she felt good after the prayer.

Girl 2

I then headed downstairs on the escalator and noticed a girl sitting at the concierge desk. I went up to the desk and explained that I was a Christian and that sometimes God points people out to me and I feel that He lets me know that He wants to tell them something.

I felt to tell her that God loved her very much and that she was extraordinarily special to Him. She teared up and indicated that she felt overwhelmed.

I explained that it must be true of her since I do not ordinarily stop and say such things to people but I explained that He pointed her out to me and wanted me to let her know. I offered to pray but she said she had to continue with something (she was quite overwhelmed) because she had a new job to start the following day and teary eyed she put her head down and got on with her 'study'.

Girl 3

I went into a hair store and was served by a girl covered in tattoos.

I again felt to say something to her so I mentioned to her that she must have amazing patience – what I felt God was showing me about her. She asked me what I meant and I replied that she must have extraordinary patience for her to sit through all that time it would have taken to get the tats – it must have taken a great deal of patience, and courage.

I then said to her that I was a Christian and that I felt that God not only let me know that she was patient and had courage but that He really 'dug her' and thought her tats were great (I wondered about this but went with it because I figured He loved her with or without them!). She then got a bit emotional and said that she needed to hear that because the day before had been the anniversary of her sister's death over twenty years ago. I said to her that my Dad had died over ten years ago but it still hurt. She agreed.

I then offered to pray for her. She agreed and I prayed quickly and she absolutely gazed into my eyes as I did it – praying just what God had said about her and how He loved her, how He thought she was great and dug her tats and that she was a girl of courage, patience, and to give her peace – I thanked God for the fact that her sister was ok.

She looked like she was ready to tear up more, but she was also very conscious that she was at work. It was very quick – she too felt God touch her.

What an amazing loving God to send me just when she needed to be loved, the day after a painful anniversary... coincidence?

66

New Christian...

R and I went to the supermarket. While collecting the groceries I saw in the corner of my eye a lady shoplifting. I questioned, why did God just allow me to see that, what am I supposed to do with that information. I wandered through the supermarket asking for guidance, asking God to help me make the right decision.

Going through the register this same lady was in front of me, she was very thin and had the appearance and energy of someone who was struggling with life. Her grocery items came to a total of around $75, she opened her wallet to pay. I stepped forward (R was thinking 'what are you doing, D?' but did not say a word). I looked at the lady and said 'I do not want you to get in trouble, but I saw what you did'. I asked her to return the goods onto the counter and I would pay for her shopping. She reached into her top and pulled out the stolen item (a big block of cheese). Her eyes filled up as she told me it was survival that made her do it and that she didn't really want to and felt terrible. I paid for her shopping. We then stepped to the side and held hands and prayed, she looked me in the eyes and said: 'you have my word I will never, ever, ever do that again'. She raised her arms in the air and wept as God touched her heart. R and I left the supermarket, got in the car and felt that 'too drunk to drive feeling'. We sat quietly and thanked the Lord for creating the unspoken mutual understanding that R and I both have; that will allow us to step forward and help others, knowing that I have R's full support and vice versa that he has mine.

OVERCOMING SIN CONSCIOUSNESS

We know that to live the normal Christian life of being like Jesus in every way we need to recognise the significance of identity theft and defeat sin consciousness. So what does the bible say about your our sin?

2 Corinthians 5:19

namely, that God was in Christ reconciling the world to Himself, not counting their trespasses against them, and He has committed to us the word of reconciliation.

As a result of Jesus' sacrifice on the cross, God is not counting **anyone's** trespass (sin) against them. There is no ledger in heaven where your sins are recorded. The 'imagined' ledger of sinfulness does not need to be balanced through dedication, spiritual discipline or commitment. This is an Old Testament concept that was changed through the work of the cross. The Kingdom of God is not a set of rules; it is a set of relationships. God is not looking to judge or condemn us; rather He is focused on the restoration of relationship. This truth is powerfully illustrated through the story of the woman caught in adultery (John 8:1–11). Relationships are not restored through threats of punishment. There is no repentance when someone is protecting the rules. Hard to believe and accept? Let's keep looking.

Colossians 2:13

When you were dead in your transgressions and the uncircumcision of your flesh, He made you alive together with Him, having forgiven us all our transgressions,

God has forgiven **all** your transgressions – past, present and future. The blood of Jesus was sufficient to forgive you and this is why anyone's sin – believer or pre-believer – is not counted against them. Your shame, guilt and self-condemnation are not necessary. Shame and fear entered the heart of man because of sin. (Genesis 3: 1–13) Yet Jesus despised the shame of the cross (Hebrews 12:2) and died naked so that we no longer have to live under the tyranny of shame, guilt and condemnation. This is truly good news! Too good for some. But wait, there's more!

Hebrews 10:11–14

Every priest stands daily ministering and offering time after time the same sacrifices, which can never take away sins; but He, having offered one sacrifice for sins for all time, sat down at the right hand of God, waiting from that time onward until his enemies be made a footstool for his feet. For by one offering He has perfected for all time those who are sanctified.

One sacrifice for sins for all time having perfected those who are sanctified. Amazingly, your standing in the sight of God after you are born again is that of a perfect son, an heir of Christ as He was the first born among many brethren. This is why Paul confidently testifies in Colossians 1:21–22

And although you were formerly alienated and hostile in mind, engaged in evil deeds, yet He has now reconciled you in His fleshly body through death, in order to present you before Him holy and blameless and beyond reproach—

If you are a follower of Jesus, God sees you as *holy, blameless* and *beyond reproach.* This is who you really are. Ephesians 1:3–7 affirms this position and relates it to being adopted as sons.

Blessed be the God and Father of our Lord Jesus Christ, who has blessed us with every spiritual blessing in the heavenly places in Christ, just as He chose us in Him before the foundation of the world, that we would be holy and blameless before Him. In love He predestined us to adoption as sons through Jesus Christ to Himself, according to the kind intention of His will, to the praise of the glory of His grace, which He freely bestowed on us in the Beloved. In Him we have redemption through His blood, the forgiveness of our trespasses, according to the riches of His grace.

This is why you can approach the throne of grace with confidence (Hebrews 4:16). You are a son of God and so you can learn to be like Jesus. This extraordinary good news is a mystery.

Colossians 1:26–27 states:

that is, the mystery which has been hidden from the past ages and generations, but has now been manifested to His saints, to whom God willed to make known what is the riches of the glory of this mystery among the Gentiles, which is Christ in you, the hope of glory.

We are one with Jesus according to Galatians 2:20

I have been crucified with Christ; and it is no longer I who live, but Christ lives in me; and the life which I now live in the flesh I live by faith in the Son of God, who loved me and gave Himself up for me.

How is this possible? It is possible because of the cross of Jesus Christ. Romans 5:18 says:

So then as through one transgression there resulted condemnation to all men, even so through one act of righteousness there resulted justification of life to all men.

Paul in Romans 3:24–26

being justified as a gift by His grace through the redemption which is in Christ Jesus; whom God displayed publicly as a propitiation in His blood through faith. This was to demonstrate

His righteousness, because in the forbearance of God He passed over the sins previously committed; for the demonstration, I say, of His righteousness at the present time, so that He would be just and the justifier of the one who has faith in Jesus.

God has passed over the sins previously committed. This act of reconciliation, justification and redemption was echoed in the book of Exodus (Chapter 12) when the angel of death passed over the houses whose door was covered in the blood of a lamb. In this context Paul writes:

'blessed is the man whose sin the lord will not take into account.' (Romans 4:8)

DEALING WITH OUR SIN

There remains the good and appropriate question of what are we to do about our sin? Clearly we are not to be sin conscious.

Even so, consider yourselves to be dead to sin, but alive to God in Christ Jesus. (Romans 6:11)

Yet it is equally clear that we can't just carry on sinning without some response.

What shall we say then? Are we to continue in sin so that grace may increase? ² May it never be! How shall we who died to sin still live in it? (Romans 6:1–2)

A study of John 16:8–11 will help us at this point.

And He, when He comes, will convict the world concerning sin and righteousness and judgment; concerning sin, because they do not believe in Me; and concerning righteousness, because I go to

the Father and you no longer see Me; and concerning judgment,
because the ruler of this world has been judged.

The Holy Spirit convicts of sin 'because they do not believe in Me'. I believe the sin that the Holy Spirit convicts people of is that of **unbelief**. The sin that separates a person from a relationship with the Father. I am unable to find any sense in the thought that the Holy Spirit convicts us of something that God is not taking into account, that He has forgiven and that He offered a sacrifice once and for all – that is, our transgressions and sin. The Father has punished and judged Jesus for all our sins. God placed all of our sin on Jesus and placed all of Jesus' righteousness on us. (2 Corinthians 5:21) Jesus identified with us at our worst so that we could be identified with Him at His best. We are righteous before God because of Jesus' actions and obedience on our behalf. This is the gift that He offers to all mankind. The gift already exists because of the death and resurrection of Jesus. Now the Father, through the Holy Spirit, is offering the opportunity to receive the gift. His offer comes with conviction of unbelief because faith is necessary to receive it (Romans 3:26).

Once the sin of unbelief is dealt with and we are reconciled to God, the Holy Spirit convicts of *'righteousness because I go to the Father and you no longer see me'* (John 16:10). Jesus is pointing to the resurrection side of the cross. Before the cross God judged and punished sin. At the cross He judged and punished Jesus for all sin for all time. The issue of sin and its place in a person's life is changed dramatically when someone believes in Jesus as Lord and Saviour. Now on the resurrection side of the cross the Father is calling His people to righteousness. God does not call His people 'out' on their sin, He calls them 'up' into who they already are.

This was the response of the prodigal son's father. That is, the father did not respond to the prodigal son's emphasis on behaviour ('I am not worthy') rather the father responded by restoring him to his 'never lost' position of being his son. God is not interested in what is wrong; He is interested in what is *missing*. The Father is not disillusioned with us, as he never had any illusions about us in the first place. In the process of calling us up, the Holy Spirit will contrast the roots of the old nature that need to be removed with the person we already are in Jesus. However at these times He is offering us freedom not judgment. Again this is why Paul calls us to be dead to sin and alive to God. (Romans 6:11) It is *what* we believe, much more than *how* we behave, that is crucial.

A consequence of eating of the tree of the knowledge of good and evil is a focus on behaviour; both our own and that of others. A focus on our own behaviour often results in sin consciousness which is then reinforced by Old Testament theology and the spirit of law and death. The net result is that we process our life with God through improving our behaviour and stopping sin.

Yet when we accept Jesus and agree with (put our faith in) what the cross accomplished we act from the tree of life. (John 14:6) What we believe about the cross connects us to the spirit of life and the New Testament emphasis on relationship. (Matthew 22:36–40) The net result is that we are now free to focus our life with God through our relationship as a son and how our beliefs impact our relationship with the Father.

The awareness of our sin presents a learning opportunity to be more like Jesus. The Spirit is saying you can move from there to here and in so doing be more like Jesus. We are being transformed into the same image from glory to glory, just as from the Lord, the Spirit. (2 Corinthians 3:18) Most importantly the awareness of sin should never be entertained as a reason to be disqualified from living as a son. Romans 5:16–17 encourages us to reign in life through Jesus.

The gift is not like that which came through the one who sinned; for on the one hand the judgment arose from one transgression resulting in condemnation, but on the other hand the free gift arose from many transgressions resulting in justification. For if by the transgression of the one, death reigned through the one, much more those who receive the abundance of grace and of the gift of righteousness will reign in life through the One, Jesus Christ.

The Holy Spirit convicts us of righteousness as it is this free gift that leads us into a knowledge of the Father.

More than that, I count all things to be loss in view of the surpassing value of knowing Christ Jesus my Lord, for whom I have suffered the loss of all things, and count them but rubbish so that I may gain Christ, and may be found in Him, not having a righteousness of my own derived from the Law, but that which is through faith in Christ, the righteousness which comes from God on the basis of faith, that I may know Him and the power of His resurrection and the fellowship of His sufferings, being conformed to His death; in order that I may attain to the resurrection from the dead. (Philippians 3:8–11)

Understanding 'righteousness' changes the way we view ourselves and this in turn affects how we engage with our life and spirituality. Somehow King David was able to see things beyond his own time and this is illustrated from Psalm 23:3:

He restores my soul;
He guides me in the paths of righteousness
For His name's sake.

The Holy Spirit wants to show us how righteous we are. Matthew 6:33 encourages us: *'But seek first His kingdom and His righteousness, and all these things will be added to you'.* Put another way, know and understand His kingdom and His righteousness and all these things will be added to you. Very few Christians have a heart-felt understanding of His righteousness and what it means for them. Without that understanding there will be limitations and restrictions in their experience as disciples of Jesus.

Further, in Romans 14:17 Paul writes: *'for the kingdom of God is not eating and drinking, but righteousness, peace and joy in the Holy Spirit.'* We can eat and drink to sustain our bodies to physically interact with life and all it brings. To sustain our spiritual lives to fully undertake the assignments we have been given to advance the kingdom of God, we need to be partaking of the qualities that righteousness, peace and joy bring to us. The free gift of righteousness helps me to reign in life (Romans 5:17), adds to my fruitfulness in God's kingdom (Romans 7:4) and positions me to live as a much loved son of God and heir with Christ (Romans 8:10–17).

Also in James 5:16(b) we find: *' the effective prayer of a righteous man can accomplish much.'* If I approach God's throne of grace with the certainty of my righteousness due to the finished work of the cross my prayers can change natural realities. Just as Jesus changed natural realities, so can I.

I love Eugene Peterson's translation in The Message of 1 John

3:18–22

My dear children, let's not just talk about love; let's practice real love. This is the only way we'll know we're living truly, living in God's reality. It's also the way to shut down debilitating self-criticism, even when there is something to it. For God is greater than our worried hearts and knows more about us than we do ourselves.

And friends, once that's taken care of and we're no longer accusing or condemning ourselves, we're bold and free before God! We're able to stretch our hands out and receive what we asked for because we're doing what he said, doing what pleases him.

Do not allow shame, guilt and condemnation to rob you or your confidence before God and the knowledge that you have the standing as a son of God and an heir of Christ Jesus. The sin that inhabited our old nature has deep roots. It is a daily work of grace to conquer it. We need Jesus to be formed in us (Galatians 4:19), but as an act of learning.

We are becoming everything we can be for Him at His pace and under the care of His coaches. Repentance is contrition for the way we have hurt the Lord. John 14:14 says: *'If you love Me, you will keep My commandments'*

A works based paradigm hears this as, if you love Me you won't mess up or do anything wrong. A grace-based paradigm hears, 'if you love Me you won't do anything to hurt me'. So repentance in the gospel of grace is saying sorry and being thankful for the forgiveness I already have and asking for insight to learn and keep walking.

In the Old Testament the Lord used judgement and tribulation to draw Israel's attention to their sin. Today Christians who reference Old Testament ways will interpret difficult times as God judging their sin. Yet Romans 5:1–5 says we have peace with God and tribulations are for our benefit, and when properly handled and interpreted lead us to the love of God.

Therefore, having been justified by faith, we have peace with God through our Lord Jesus Christ, through whom also we have obtained our introduction by faith into this grace in which we stand; and we exult in hope of the glory of God. And not only this, but we also exult in our tribulations, knowing that tribulation brings about perseverance; and perseverance, proven character; and proven character, hope; and hope does not disappoint, because the love of God has been poured out within our hearts through the Holy Spirit who was given to us.

So, the Holy Spirit convicts pre-believers of unbelief because the Father longs to be reconciled to all men (2 Corinthians 5:18 – 21). The Holy Spirit convicts believers of their righteousness so that they learn to walk in what the cross was for them. Then the Holy Spirit convicts believers concerning judgment because the ruler of this world, Satan has been judged. The Father wants believers to undertake life's battles from the position that 'the victory has been won'. This points to matters of influence and inheritance that will be covered in the next chapter.

FEAR OF THE LORD AND JUDGEMENT

As I come to conclude my thoughts on the 'new thing' we have received called identity, it is appropriate to address the place of the fear of the Lord and matters of judgement in the New Testament. We need to know the fear of the Lord (2 Corinthians 5:11) understanding that it is a terrifying thing to fall into the hands of a living God. We who believe in Him are not judged (John 3:18) and having received the abundance of grace and the gift of righteousness will reign in life (Romans 5:16–17). Yet, we are judged by the law of liberty (James 2:12) and need to pay attention to our words (Matthew 12:36), our attitudes (Matthew 7:1–2), our judgement of others (James 5:9) and our fruitfulness (2 Corinthians 5:10).

This issue of what the Lord judges and its impact on our relationship with Him as a Father, not a judge, is highlighted in the parable of the ten virgins (Matthew 25:1–13). A student in our college captured the tension between Father and judge when she asked: 'How does the parable of the ten virgins relate to grace and the issue of not slipping back into a performance or works-based mindset of striving to hang onto our salvation?'

I posed this question to my friend Allan Meyer. His response is worth including here for the benefit of all:

> The book of James addresses the issue I believe Jesus addressed in the parable of the Ten Bridesmaids. I think the issue it addresses is this:
>
> *1:19-22 'Know this, my beloved brothers; let every person be quick to hear, slow to speak, slow to anger; for the anger of man does not produce the righteousness of God. Therefore put away all filthiness*

and rampant wickedness and receive with meekness the implanted word, which is able to save your souls. But be doers of the word, and not hearers only, deceiving yourselves.'

2:14 'What good is it, my brothers, if a man claims to have faith but has no deeds?'

2:18 'Show me your faith without deeds, and I will show you my faith by what I do. You believe that there is one God. Good! Even the demons believe that - and shudder.'

The Parable of the Ten Bridesmaids is built on the understanding of the practice of Jewish weddings. The bride invited her friends to help her get ready for her wedding. The ten virgins are in fact ten bridesmaids. This is an insight not found in the other parables about a wedding – you can be a guest at a wedding and have no responsibility to help make the wedding happen. That's how we view an invitation to a wedding - I'm invited, I go, they do the wedding, I watch and congratulate and all is well. This parable adds an important insight to the process. A bridesmaid is a guest with responsibilities. A bridesmaid has the responsibility to help make the wedding happen. That's us. We are not just invited to a wedding – we are called to partner with God in making the wedding happen.

The key responsibility of a bridesmaid was around the torchlight parade. The wedding did not happen at a precise time. It would happen at the bridegroom's house or the father of the bridegroom's house. When all was ready, usually at night, the bridesmaids would provide a torchlight parade back to the house where the wedding would take place. Ten were invited. Five embraced their responsibility and five did not. Those five are reminiscent of those Jesus refers to in other places – did we not cast out demons, do miracles – 'I don't know you.'

The sober warning of this parable is: 'don't deceive yourself'. Hearing the word and embracing the word are two different things. You only know you are embracing the word as you observe yourself taking the word seriously – you make different choices, you do things differently. To act as if obedience is in some way disconnected from faith is to demonstrate a lack of understanding of what faith is. Faith = I hear, I accept, I embrace. To hear, to accept but not embrace is to deceive yourself – and at this point behaviour plays its vital role of revealing what I (and you) really believe.

Five bridesmaids accepted their invitation, knew there was a wedding, would like to be a guest, but never embraced their discipleship responsibility to help make the wedding happen. They were not graced – they were self-deceived. By grace we are saved through faith, and that not of yourselves, by gift of God, not of works, lest any man should boast. YES. BUT, faith has sleeves rolled up as it embraces the word.

It's all by grace. Behaviour reveals whether grace has landed or you are only deceiving yourself.

That's my understanding of this parable – which by the way I preached earlier this year and had exactly these questions raised by troubled listeners who were seeking to build their base on grace and found this message a little confronting. I think the New Testament is confronting. Above the line –GRACE. Below the line – BEHAVIOUR. Just keep the emphasis on grace, and use behaviour as a thermometer for and indicator of reality over self-deception.

Scripture encourages us to judge ourselves or we can expect the Lord's discipline (1 Corinthians 11:31–32). The Lord disciplines those who he loves (Revelation 3:19) and when we are living as sons, He disciplines us as a father (Hebrews 12:7). It is good for us to be disciplined because it leads to us sharing in His holiness and yields the peaceful fruit of righteousness. Yet, when Old Testament theology informs New Testament living, discipline can be interpreted and experienced as judgement of sin. The Lord clearly tests our faith (1 Peter 1:7) for the purpose of being yielded and surrendered to Him so that we can walk in the works He has prepared for us (Ephesians 2:10). God's focus in both discipline and testing is on our sanctification (Hebrews 12:14) so that we might discover the narrow path (Matthew 7:14) and see Him in all His glory (Hebrews 12:14). For those of us who believe in Jesus we do not come into judgement for our sin (John 5:24) but the Lord does expect us to work with Him to be changed from glory to glory.

Hence Peter writes,

Now for this very reason also, applying all diligence, in your faith supply moral excellence, and in your moral excellence, knowledge, (2 Peter 1:5)

We are to supply moral excellence to our faith. Character is important. However we supply moral excellence from the wisdom of the law not the condemnation of the law. Paul also writes,

But if the ministry of death, in letters engraved on stones, came with glory, so that the sons of Israel could not look intently at the face of Moses because of the glory of his face, fading as it was, how will the ministry of the Spirit fail to be even more with glory? For

if the ministry of condemnation has glory, much more does the ministry of righteousness abound in glory. For indeed what had glory, in this case has no glory because of the glory that surpasses it. For if that which fades away was with glory, much more that which remains is in glory. (2 Corinthians 3: 7-11)

All too often God's people allow the law to condemn them. In the New Testament the place of the law that was fulfilled in Jesus, is for wisdom to know what to choose, so as to live in a way that honours God.

A significant key to raising up and making disciples who see the normal Christian life as being like Jesus in every way is to help them accept and live from their identity in Jesus. That is to be son conscious. There are two enemies of being son conscious: firstly, the draw on our soul to be sin conscious; and, secondly the role identity theft and how it has played in our understanding of what it is to be human. The gospel of grace, rightly proclaimed, results in being son conscious. The gospel of works ultimately results in law and can only propagate sin consciousness and promulgate identity theft.

I can be like Jesus in every way because I am a son of God. I am as righteous as Jesus because I live in His righteousness. As heaven invaded earth through Jesus it can also invade through me because Christ is in me, the hope of glory.

Let's hear more stories from disciples who are living like Jesus lived.

Chair leads to prayer and healing...

I work with the elderly and disabled. On going to a client's home Tuesday morning to assess her chair, I noticed she had arm braces on and has a great deal of trouble touching anything due to arthritis in her wrists and arms. Long story short, I asked her could I pray for her because God doesn't like to see his children sick. Her daughter was there and they said they believed in God, I sat her down and asked her daughter to join with me and I prayed for her mum. Well it was a simple prayer; I left the house with her old chair and prayed for her as I was driving around again.

I had to get approval for a new chair from the Government as it was over the limit for funding so I rang the dept and they said to send in a quote as usual and go through the process. This was not to be, as I rang back the funding body later in the day to advice that I had located a chair for this lady at a cheaper price. They gave me instant approval over the phone at the higher price which was unusual; not only that, but when I picked up the chair at the manufacturers the chair was cheaper than I was quoted so in a nut shell I got more than I asked for and paid less than I was quoted.

Getting back to the lady, I returned on this Thursday to deliver her new chair and as I was setting it up for her I noticed that she had no braces on I asked her what happened to them, She said that she forgot to tell me, that after I prayed and had left, all the pain left her and now she doesn't need the braces. She was waving her arms and twisting her wrists around. I asked her what else do you want, and I prayed for that as well.

She had an incredible smile on her face and her other daughter and Auntie were there as well which gave me opportunity to speak about God's love for us and then prayed for the mother again with the daughter; the Auntie asked me to keep coming back to see them. I am going back next week to see what else God has done in her life and family. All I had to do was open my mouth. God did the rest, very humbling.

83

Gift of healing for the wrapper of gifts...

I was driving to my daughter's home about two weeks ago with the intention of having coffee at the local shops in Mt Waverley. As I neared her home, a picture of the shopping strip at Albert Park came to mind. We prayed and were open to what God might want so we drove to Albert Park and began to wander and browse in the stores. All the while, I was seeking to hear what God might be saying. Our time was up (the parking meter was about to expire) but we went into one more store.

The woman behind the counter told us she had sold her store two days ago after being in business 25 years. She went on to explain she'd developed arthritis, fibromyalgia and some other condition I don't remember. This left her with hands as stiff as a board, purple in colour and icy cold. She could only move them slightly with much pain and difficulty, the circulation was 'dying' (her words).She went on to explain how there were no answers and it broke her heart to sell her livelihood but she could no longer wrap gifts which was a core part of her business at Christmas.

By this time I knew she was the reason I found myself in Albert Park for only the second time in my life! I told her I was a Christian and believed God heals today the same as he did 2000 years ago. I asked if I might pray and she readily agreed. I prayed and Jesus healed her!

I asked her to do something she couldn't previously do. She bent her fingers and said the pain (previously an 8/10) was gone. She complained of some stiffness so I prayed again. She was delighted and began to ask for details of our church and what had happened to her. She picked up a pen while she was distracted. Upon realising she was holding the pen, she was amazed and overwhelmed as she hadn't been able to do this for some time.

My daughter and I left the store knowing we'd accomplished the task God had for us and returned to our expired parking meter with no fine!

And he played footy that Saturday...

It was mid-Winter 2009 and I was driving with my then 2-year-old son to school to collect my daughter. It was smack in the middle of the Aussie Rules football season and in typical Melbourne style it was raining a drizzly type rain.

As I drove I saw a stay at home Dad that I had got to know called M. He was walking to school in the rain. M is a rough gem who wears shorts and thongs or runners all year round (winter and summer), and who had got many of the women's tongues wagging up at the school for his lack of charm... in other words he called a spade a spade... and I liked him...

I pulled over and offered him a ride. He responded by saying that that normally he would say no, but that on this day he would say yes because he had hurt his knee. He jumped into the car and we rode the short distance to school, chatting as we went. I asked about the knee and he said that it was an old injury that required a knee reconstruction. By the time we were in the playground waiting for the kids to come out I knew I had to offer to pray, but did not know how to do it with him in front of all the other mums at school pick up.

God had given me a picture, and I had just learnt that God will sometimes give us a picture of how He wants us to pray to release a healing. The picture I had received was that I was to kneel down in front of him and place my hand on his bare knee and pray as I knelt.

I offered to pray. M said he did not believe in any of **that** stuff but that I could give it a go if I wanted. He then went on to say that if it worked it would be great to be able to play football that Saturday... but he doubted it would work.

I did not want to kneel – it was wet on the ground, he was a man wearing shorts and I felt it was inappropriate to kneel in front of him in the wet with my hand on his bare knee... and, what was worse, it was in front of all the other mums, milling around waiting for their kids to come out of school!

So, in **my** 'wisdom' I placed my hand discreetly on his shoulder and started to pray. As I prayed I felt/heard a strong rebuke from God who said 'Get on your knees' – essentially saying I showed you how to pray, now do it'.

I took a deep breath, focusing on the fact that M could be healed, and told him that I needed to place my hand on his knee. And so I knelt in the wet, with the cold and wet coming through my jeans, in front of the car park mums and prayed. The mums looked at me and I felt very embarrassed, but went on regardless.

While on my knees, feeling very vulnerable, I looked up at him and asked if he felt anything – he said he felt heat and so I kept praying and then asked him to move the knee around... he did and he felt some relief so I prayed again, still on my knees and I then stood and asked him to try it out...

He bent it back and forth and said all the pain was gone. I asked him to jump on it, jumping up and down next to him as I did. He jumped up and down on it and looked amazed and said there was no more pain and that he would not have believed it... but that he had felt the heat and that it was amazing, that maybe he was wrong about all this stuff...

Delighted (and that is an understatement!), I got on with collecting my daughter and left it at that...

I saw him the following week and asked how he had got on. He said, like a little kid, with absolute joy, that he had played his game of footy that Saturday!

CHAPTER THREE
WHAT CAN I EXPECT?

Sin blocked the path to union with God. Since we could not come to God, He came to us. The cross represented Christ as the victor not the victim.

God came close to us to make us. We were handmade and He stood face to face to breathe life into us (Genesis 1: 27). God called us to live in His image. We were created for friendship. God called us to live in His likeness (Genesis 1:26). We can move in the same attitudes and ways; in unity, love, generosity, power. God called us to live with authority over the earth (Genesis 1: 28). We are created to expand and fill the earth with His kingdom. God comes down to our level to lift us up to His.

When man fell in sin, He who loves us could not stay at a distance. Jesus did not come to make bad people good. Jesus came to make natural people supernatural. We are new creations and we are a new race of people who are divine. John 1:12 declares: 'but as many as received Him, to them He gave the right to become children of God, even to those who believe in His name.' He has restored our ability to live in heavenly realms while here on earth. In John 3, Nicodemus is told on our behalf that when we are born again we are born from above. We are planted in heaven. We are no longer outsiders but insiders.

The Holy Spirit wants to stir our affections for His world, and also the unseen, more than this world. We are to agree with heaven to draw heaven to earth and see our words become spirit. We are to pursue revelation for encounters with God, not just knowledge. Jesus' worth makes us worthy to receive assignments that require power from heaven to confront the works of the devil.

God did not put His Spirit in us to do church and administer programmes. We are filled with the Spirit to live in the spiritual climate that surrounds us. If I am focussed on the natural realm; that is, my work, my effort, my responsibility or what others think, it is like being on the AM band on the radio. If I am focussed on engaging the spirit realm; that is, the ways of God, what He is saying, how I am learning to join myself to Him, then I am on the FM band of the radio. When I am on the AM band I cannot receive the FM band, but when I do receive it, the flow of what God is releasing is amazing. I trust the following stories thrill your heart as they do mine.

Healing from breast cancer...

I would like to thank you both (two Stairway staff members) sincerely from the bottom of my heart upwards for your prayer ministry for my recent BreastScreen further assessment. I will enclose the original follow up letter from BreastScreen Victoria.

I was concerned because my mother and sister both had breast cancer and was scared of the genetic links and high probability of myself having breast cancer.

These are the dates and events that followed after I received the letter on 20/2/2012 from BreastScreen Victoria.

I rang JC and left a message on her answering machine at church.

On February 22nd JC rang me back and prayed for me across the phone. She declared heaven come to earth filled with love, joy, peace and the power of Jesus healing flowing through me. That there would be no cancer cells or calcification in my breasts now or in the future. At that stage I didn't know what the follow up assessment had found on my original mammogram.

I went to 48HOP* and asked for prayer, as I was not sleeping and still feeling anxious. CC came and prayed for me. I explained I had prayer but needed more. She prayed for me and had a vision of God lifting a huge rock off me, it was a huge burden. I have been going through all sorts of trials recently; my mother passed away and I have been going to help my father with household duties and felt grief, stress and exhaustion over having to carry most of the load helping him. I was looking forward in 2012 to applying for a job and getting on with my life and then I received correspondence from BreastScreen for a follow up assessment. C prayed for God's healing and peace over my whole situation and By His Stripes I am Healed.

BreastScreen rang me on Wednesday 29th February to let me know my appointment was Tuesday 6th March 2012 at St Vincent's BreastScreen and they had found a small mass of calcification cells on my right breast.

On Sunday, 4th March Peter was leading the 6pm service; I then had prayer with C after the service. She again saw a vision of a boulder being removed from a river that was stopping water flowing around it. The water started flowing again, bubbling up and filling out on all sides. We declared that no calcification in the future or cancer cells to grow and declared joy to overflow in me. She also saw Jesus holding my hand as I go to the appointment on the day.

Yesterday, Tuesday 6th March I awoke with the song in my head played at Sunday pm service: His Love Never Runs Out, and I felt at peace. I was driving to my girlfriend's place and a car bumper sticker in front of me said 'All things are possible with God'. I declared that for myself today.

I had met the Breast Care Nurse who explained the process and what they had found on the original mammogram and said I had to have a biopsy today and will be in the high risk of getting breast cancer in future. I started to sweat as I was scared to have a biopsy, but inside of my mind I stated: 'By His Stripes I Am Healed.'

I had two further mammograms and the radiologist said she could see the original lump, but no lump on my new mammograms; she had to speak to the surgeon to get his further approval. I started to get excited. I had to wait to see the surgeon as he had to examine the original mammogram from 2nd February 2012 and compare it with today's mammograms.

The surgeon said I was clear and that I wasn't in the high risk category because there appears no calcification on my breast. He asked me how I felt. I said RELIEVED and had a huge smile on my face. (Understatement!)

* 48 HOP (Hours of Prayer) is an annual prayer initiative at Stairway which provides various creative and interactive means to connect with God.

Migraine defeated and player gets back in the game...

My son's coach said her son had a migraine so I offered to pray for him – wasn't so hard as they were Christians [but still takes guts!]; however I wasn't sure how the young fourteen-year old might take to me laying hands on him, so I asked him and he agreed. As I sat there in the stadium, fully conscious that those around us were probably wondering what on earth I was doing, I proceeded to bow my head and pray – again the sensation came on me and again just moving my hands commanded the migraine to leave and asked God to heal him completely.

When I finished praying I asked if he felt better, he said 'a bit'. I said, 'don't worry God will fix it for you'. At that time my son came over having broken his glasses. While I was trying to sticky tape the glasses back together the coach's son suddenly declares: 'it's totally gone – Mum sub me on!'... for the rest of the day he was fantastic.

Every attempt is a success – God rewards risks, not outcomes...

I am finally writing a testimony for you!! I was walking into a shopping centre and a guy walking towards me had a brace on his foot. I stopped him and asked what happened – he had put a crow bar through his foot and broken two toes.

I told him I was a Christian and asked would he mind if I prayed for it. He was blown away and proceeded to tell me that he was a Catholic but didn't go to church, but his Mum did. He had just had his second daughter christened on the weekend and couldn't understand how the Catholic

Church could be in so much turmoil with scandals etc. and didn't really like the church. I said the Church (body of Christ) had got it wrong for so long keeping their beliefs and traditions within the four walls of the church and that God wanted a relationship with His people, not religion, which kept people in bondage.

I said that I went to a church that was committed to taking the good news of the gospel out into the streets, homes, schools, wherever we go and releasing the Kingdom of Heaven into people's lives through love and prayer and practical acts of kindness, just like Jesus. I told him how exciting church is and how the kids are taught and how God is using kids in mighty ways and he should consider coming and experiencing the presence of God in a church that is on fire for God. He was really touched that someone would take the time to stop and pray for him. I prayed for his toes and asked him if he felt anything. He said he didn't but that didn't bother me. I know it was God's timing and he was clearly touched. And who knows what God did on his way home, not just in his foot, but in his heart and mind?

God assists the assistants...

Then I went to Chaddy (shopping centre) and while I was in Myer a lady very kindly helped me in the children's department. She was very honest and caring and took time to really help me. There was nothing there that interested me and as I was thanking her for her great service I felt very strongly to pray for her. I told her I was a Christian and asked if there was anything she would like prayer for. She just stood there stunned and staring at me and finally said, "I have been praying to God for help and direction as I have a big decision to make. She was delighted that I would pray and so I did. She felt God's peace come and I encouraged her with what the word says and how much God loved her.

Then I went to pick up a cake for my mums 80th from the cake shop I usually go to, and the assistant gave me all these free yummy Italian patisserie cakes! As I was thanking her and telling her she could expect a blessing from God for being so kind, she said, 'I need all the blessing I can get at the moment'.' I sensed to reach out and pray for her so I held her hand and prayed a blessing over her and you could feel God's presence. She was teary. There were other customers waiting so I had to go, but I said I would be happy to pray for her any time and she was really touched that someone cared enough to pray. I sense in my spirit she will come to church one day. Yay God.

CHANGING OUR VIEW OF THE NORMAL CHRISTIAN LIFE

To live a normal Christian life is to be like Jesus in every way. His food was to do the will of *'Him who sent Me'* (John 3:34). He was concerned to do what He saw the Father doing (John 5:19). He understood He was empowered by the Spirit and that we also need that same empowerment in order to be disciples (John 14:17). I'm wondering what your view of the normal Christian life is and whether you are a disciple in the way I am describing. Certainly seven years ago I was not! So what has helped the process of transition for me and others?

A movie was released in 2011 in called "The Help". It is set in the state of Mississippi in the 1960s against the backdrop of the American civil rights movement. Young, white American women who are married with children employ older African-American women as maids. The maids are referred to as 'the help'.

The young, white women have predominantly grown up together in a town in the Deep South. One of their number has been to New York to study journalism and is returning home as a single woman looking for employment. She, like her friends, had grown up in homes with maids. However, upon her return she begins to questions the prejudice her friends have towards their black servants. She is enraged by the injustice 'the help' experience and decides to document their stories.

One of the themes of the movie is how both the white and African-American women are captives of the culture they have grown up in. Their expectations have been shaped by the historic values of slavery. While 'the help' know they are suffering injustice they are afraid to challenge the status quo because they fear they will lose their jobs.

The catalyst for change is the white girl who had studied in New York. She returns to her home town with a different perspective. She now sees 'the help' as people with hopes, dreams and aspirations like their white employers. Her change of perspective leads her to encourage 'the help' to change the way they view themselves. At the same time, she begins to influence her peers to examine their perception of 'the help' and in turn, themselves. As the issue of identity is addressed, tension and conflict escalate to damaging levels and there will be chaos before a new, more equitable, order, is created.

In a way, it is easier to see order in the past, and to lament for the 'good old days'. In the 1930s and 40's, for example, it seemed as if most people accepted their place and identity. Change has occurred since, and now, nearly seventy years on, there is a new order and identity making its presence known in the world, to the point where America elected the first African-American president, Barack Obama. Living through transition is chaotic, painful, destabilising and potentially destructive. However, handled well, transition releases new life.

Our transition at Stairway into the understanding that the normal Christian life is to live like Jesus in every way, needed to take place primarily in our belief systems. We have had to allow the Holy Spirit and the Word of God to invade our core. Life with God and in His kingdom invariably progresses through His work in our hearts. (Ezekiel 36:26)

As we have allowed the Lord to lead us into this understanding of the normal Christian life, we have needed to:

- be strong and courageous in embracing new ways;
- live in humility so that the seeds of change had fertile soil to flourish in;
- adopt a constant stance of faith as we learned how to invade the impossible with God;
- relish the opportunity for reinvention, recognising that it allows us to advance the kingdom of God;
- embrace forgiveness as some around us make mistakes in their exploration of this new way; and,
- persevere and keep walking through the disappointments and apparent failures in our attempts to be like Jesus in every way.

Equally to stay on the journey together, we have had to develop our commitment to:

- loving the learning and not make setbacks personal;
- promoting and developing unity of heart and purpose through an attitude of honour towards all;
- being focussed on what we are becoming and encouraging one another to look to what will be;
- paying attention to how we show up in the chaos of transition, particularly where there is tension, conflict and discouragement;

- living by priorities, not reacting to pressure; and,
- managing our energy more than managing our time, so that through a love-based relationship with the Lord our output does not exceed our input.

In the transition we have had to learn to live from places of rest and peace, avoiding the temptation to struggle and strive. It is our relationship with Jesus that is the key. John 15:5–7 are clear:

I am the vine, you are the branches; he who abides in Me and I in him, he bears much fruit, for apart from Me you can do nothing. If anyone does not abide in Me, he is thrown away as a branch and dries up; and they gather them, and cast them into the fire and they are burned. If you abide in Me, and My words abide in you, ask whatever you wish, and it will be done for you.

We are to be so filled with His presence and goodness that we 'leak' Him. It is His goodness, not mine, that others need. It is what He has done not what I am doing that will make a difference. God is good at what He does. All He needs from us is to recognise that He wants to show up where we are. We are to seek and carry His presence through our hearts, knowing that hunger never goes unnoticed in the kingdom. We are learning to partner with what we already have through grace. For example, my job is not to get sick people healed. My job is to hang out with Jesus, the one who is healing, and see Him heal the sick.

Our zeal and passion can take us into places of struggle and striving. The danger here is that we leave the domain of relationship with God and enter into the realm of religion. Religion tries to convince us that we lack something we already have. Religion comes from pursuing, in our own way or strength, something we already have. We see this work of the evil one in Eve's story.

Eve was created in the image of God. Yet the devil's temptation hinged on Eve being able to *be* like God if she ate of the fruit. Eve needlessly tried to gain something she already had through another way. A pointless activity. Similarly the evil one approached Jesus and challenged who He already was, the Son of God. He tempted Jesus to reach, through His own efforts, for what was already His.

It interests me that in Luke 3:22 the Father says to Jesus, '*You are my beloved Son...*' When the devil tempts Jesus he says, '*If you are the Son of God...*', but there is a key word missing in the devil's temptation – 'beloved'. The experiences and encounters we have with God's love (Ephesians 3:19) are central to keeping us reliant on God's grace. When we are unsure in our hearts of God's love for us we will serve Him to gain love or feel loved. This approach only takes us into the law and a works-based faith/spirituality. When we are sure in our hearts of God's love for us we serve Him from love and co-labour with Him through grace. I would maintain that when John wrote about himself as, 'the disciple whom Jesus loved' (John 13:23, 19:26, 20:2, 21:7, 21:20) he was not being arrogant or singling himself out. Rather, he was helping the reader understand the significance of knowing that each of us is *personally* loved by Jesus. It is, after all, the key to being fuelled up with the fullness of God (Ephesians 3:19).

We continue to see the changed lives that our journey together is releasing. Here are a few more stories.

Change in the atmosphere...

I've visited Stairway at different times over the years but recently my husband and I decided to come on a more regular basis and then made the choice to be permanent, so we've been floating here for about two months now. One of the things that's impacted me has been the atmosphere, it's like the church is on a different spiritual level to what I've experienced before. And I've found whoever I'm with or have had dialogue with at the church, there's just an atmosphere of ACCEPTANCE, THE ATMOSPHERE IS - WE ACCEPT YOU, IT'S OKAY TO BE YOU, AND WHATS MORE WE WANT YOU TO BE YOU AND WE WANT TO ENCOURAGE AND HELP YOU IN THAT. Wow!

Within myself I've relaxed a lot more and as a result I'm accepting myself more, and because God's love is able to flow through me more easily I'm then able to love and accept people with a lot more ease myself. It's a very different and new thing to experience that. Its like there's no Works, Striving, etc.... there's just a confidence in knowing God's love and passing that love on. I'm really appreciating it because I feel loved in a way I haven't been before, and I think I feel freer and less inhibited being around people because of that. Anyway just to share and say thank you.

I know there would have been a lot of emptying out on behalf of everyone here at Stairway in order for that atmosphere to be created. You know, Religion, Rules, Regulations, Expectations, Legalism, Obligations etc.... - all have to go in order to come into a TRUE AND LOVING RELATIONSHIP WITH GOD AND THEREFORE WITH EACH OTHER.

It seems I've just walked in on the cusp of things, when that clearing out, putting everything on the altar before God, all that work has been done and I get to enjoy the ride of the fruit of all that hard work.

Thank you, and thank you to Stairway for creating an amazing God dwelling and loving environment.

Relationship change...

Thanks for fire starters this term. This leaves me ready to go forward now rather than in four more weeks. There have been many changes in my life as a result of fire starters, none bigger than the last week's message about accepting God as my Heavenly Father, and the Holy Spirit as the maternal influence, as for so many of us this wasn't great for me. I was stuck in thinking that forgiving them was enough for me to go forward. I have always understood my relationship with Jesus, and that on its own has been amazing, I listened to your words on Sunday and found what I had let hold me back for so long in my relationship with my earthly parents and have spent the last few days with this working through this. Already feeling the massive change in my heart and can't wait to see what happens next.

More than a movie...

Went to see a movie at Southland with a Christian friend... saw a wheelchair at first and knowing my friend wouldn't be so enthusiastic I chickened out (**from praying for the occupant**.)

Then we were at Grill'd and a girl walks in with crutches! This time I couldn't back down (crutches of course being less intimidating... ha ha!). I sat and finished my burger telling God, 'ok, once she goes and sits down I'll go over'.

After all the thoughts of fear that ran through my mind there was nothing left to do but have faith!!! This year I asked God to help me break through the freezing-up zone...

So, I told my friend, I'm going to go pray for that girl – she casually replies, 'ok'.

Now I really had to do it!!!!

Once I was ready I left my friend at our table and I said 'I'm going in', just as the girl was getting all romantic and in close conversation with her boyfriend. I quickly asked if I could interrupt for a moment and asked her what happened to her knee... she said she fell off a wall and that possibly her ligaments were twisted. She looked at me strangely asking..."why?"

I told her I go to a church where people pray for others and we see a lot of healings take place. I asked if she minded if I prayed for her, adding that it wouldn't do any harm praying. She said 'sure!'

She let me gently lay my hand on her knee as I prayed for healing. After I finished I asked if she felt anything. She said no but that if she is healed she will thank me... I said to her that she could wake up tomorrow healed and that she should thank God!

She was very open and I was thrilled I had stepped out again!!! I was so excited at the possibility of her being healed... it was so worth it!!!! I felt I had broken through a barrier in my faith level also... hallelujah!!!! God is GOOD!

It got me excited to pray for more... cheers

When the normal Christian life is to be like Jesus in every way, settling the matter of identity is crucial. To date, we have discovered that the other equally significant matter to embrace is that of friendship with Jesus or *intimacy*. Our intimacy with Jesus, to be like Him in every way, can only be built on the heart experience of knowing we are personally loved by Him. The encounter I had with God's love, as described in *A Voyage of Mercy*, changed everything for me. The best summary of those changes is found in Diagram 3.

PARADIGM OF ACCEPTANCE	PARADIGM OF PERFORMANCE
Work *from* love	Work *for* love
His business:	**My business:**
• What is He saying and doing	• Being in control
• Faith and obedience	• Avoiding fear
• Concern for signs and wonders	• Concern for reputation
• Whose presence matters	• Who is present
• How do I get to enter God's world	• How do I get God to enter my world
What's first for Him:	**What's first for me:**
• Being	• Doing
• Obedience	• Being right
• Vulnerable & weak	• Gifts & abilities
• Grace	• Activity
My focus is on / I care about:	**My focus is on / I care about:**
• His majesty	• Outcomes
• His power	• Opinions
• His promises	• Self
• His life	• Safety
Outcomes	**Outcomes:**
• God's love defined by revelation	• God's love defined by circumstances
• Faith in nature & character of God	• Sight is activated over faith

DIAGRAM 3

Over time, I learned to live out of acceptance and from love. I longed to bring this revelation to every aspect of what it meant to be a disciple. I loved serving God, but looking back, I can see that the Spirit was inviting me into a place of being a disciple where sonship with the Father and friendship with the Spirit was more important. I valued church meetings and the fellowship of small groups, but I now see the Spirit was drawing me back to the place of power encounters I had experienced in my conversion as a hallmark of what a disciple of Jesus can expect. I had become a disciple of the church culture I was raised in and recruited others to serve my vision as leader; however I intuitively knew I was missing something.

As I reflect upon that time I can see the Spirit was beginning to open my eyes to see that disciples are free men in Christ who have their own assignments to fulfil, often beyond the life of the church I led. As a leader I was becoming restless for those I was leading to have their own experiences of God's love and to build a community of disciples who were empowered to be like Jesus in every way.

IS GOD FATHER OR JUDGE?

Many of God's people live with an unconscious confusion around who God is for them today. In the Garden of Eden God was a Father to Adam and Eve. He walked in the cool of the evening with them, celebrating life and love with them. When they ate of the fruit of the tree of the knowledge of good and evil they had sinned. Yet, even though God knew this, He entered the garden that day as a Father. He was seeking a conversation with them. He did not storm into the garden with anger and fury looking to condemn and punish them.

God was placed in the role of judge while always maintaining the heart of a Father. This is why mercy will triumph over judgement. The role of the judge is to protect the integrity of something. Adam and Eve's sin meant that God had to protect the integrity of the tree of life and His redemptive plan for the human race. He judged their behaviour to protect the eternal future of mankind.

The Old Testament consistently reveals God predominantly as a judge. The Ten Commandments define His relationship with man on the basis of behaviour. The promise of blessing following obedience and cursing (judgement) following disobedience reinforces the connection between behaviour and the role of a judge. Yet when Jesus walked on the earth, one of His primary purposes was to restore the image of God from judge to Father.

During His time with the disciples He created a fascination about God within their ranks. This fascination bubbles out of Philip when he asks, *'Lord show us the Father, and it is enough for us'* (John 14:8). As Old Testament believers they were familiar with the image of God as judge. This is evidenced by James and John's response when Jesus was not received by a village of Samaritans (Luke 9:51–56). History told them that the response of God was to punish those who rejected Him, thus their first response was: 'Lord, do you want us to command fire to come down from heaven and consume them?' Jesus was facilitating a breaking down of their perception of God from judge and re-introducing Him to them as a loving Father.

Jesus responded to Philip by saying 'if you have seen Me you have seen the Father.' Jesus was kind and forgiving to sinners; He did not stand in judgment of them. This thought is further illustrated by Jesus' response to the question, 'Lord teach us to pray'. He begins with 'Our Father' not 'Our Judge'. To our ears it seems ridiculous to pray to a judge. However, for the disciples, as Old Testament believers, to pray to God as a Father would have felt equally unnatural.

In this context I am intrigued by Mary's conversation with Jesus at His tomb:

Jesus said to her, 'Stop clinging to Me, for I have not yet ascended to the Father; but go to My brethren and say to them, "'I ascend to My Father and your Father, and My God and your God.'" (John 20:17)

The first thing Jesus wants to affirm to His disciples is that they are relating to God as a Father. The propensity we have of relating to God as judge and not Father comes easily as a consequence of the brokenness of our hearts and the prevalence of Old Testament theology and religion. This idea of God as judge is further reinforced if our natural fathers were inclined to stand in judgment of our weaknesses and shortcomings. Our culture rewards performance so strongly that there is an inexorable pull towards judgment of self and others. The tree of the knowledge of good and evil has wired us for judgment. There is a prevailing thought that we get what we deserve.

Yet the story of the prodigal son (Luke 15:11–32), as discussed earlier in the book, deeply challenges all these stereotypes. To his father, he was not a son on the basis of deeds, or worth, but by birth and blood.

As followers of Jesus we are brought near to the Father by the blood of Jesus (Ephesians 2:13). Trying to be worthy to be a son is illegitimate and unnecessary. Jesus preached peace, not judgment, to bring us near (Ephesians 2:17) and provide relationship with the Father (Ephesians 2:18). God has honoured us by elevating our status from sinner to friend. He wants us to learn that we are people of spirit and grace, not judgment.

Following the resurrection we can always approach God as Father because all our sins have been judged and forgiven (Hebrews 10:11–14:2, Corinthians 5:19, Colossians 2:13). He gives good gifts to His children (Matthew 7:7–11) and we can approach His throne with confidence (Hebrews 4:16) because His is Father not judge. God judged Jesus so we could approach Him as Father:

He made Him who knew no sin to be sin on our behalf, so that we might become the righteousness of God in Him. (2 Corinthians 5:21)

I have three children; the youngest is my son David. He is married to Christy and is a fine young man who loves God and people. I am very proud of him as I am of his two sisters. However, when Davey was fifteen he was still discovering his way in life. He was uncertain about his place in the world. This resulted in him behaving badly at school. He acted in a way he now regrets but at the time he essentially violated elements of the school's code of conduct.

When I was told what he had done, my first instinct as a loving father was not to punish him. I knew the school would act as judge. I knew there needed to be consequences for his inappropriate behaviour. However, foremost in my heart was to help him see why he had behaved this way, what he could do to change and to call him up into being the person I really believed he was and wanted to be.

As Christians we are reconciled to God and He calls us up into righteousness. He does not call us out on our sin to punish or judge us. He judged Jesus so that He could be Father to us. There may be natural consequences flowing from our choices and behaviour. However God is a Father who longs for sons who are friends and who trust Him. John 5:19 records Jesus saying:

> *Therefore Jesus answered and was saying to them, "Truly, truly, I say to you, the Son can do nothing of Himself, unless it is something He sees the Father doing; for whatever the Father does, these things the Son also does in like manner.*

To be like Jesus in every way presupposes a relationship with the Father that is full of life, joy, love, peace and certainty of His goodness. It is a relationship so precious that a disciple of Jesus will do whatever is necessary to remain close to the one who is loved (John 15:5, 1 John 4:16). Disciples of Jesus co-labour with the godhead because they are convinced through encounter and experience that God is a Father who loves unconditionally and is no longer the judge of the Mosaic covenant.

Here are some more stories to inspire you:

Realigned spine...

I also wanted to let you know that I prayed for one of the people who comes to my Tuesday lunchtime prayer group at work (there are three of us who have been attending regularly for over a year). My colleague said his back was very sore and his spine was curving incorrectly. I prayed and encouraged another person to pray too and lay hands (I don't think she's laid hands before) and the man we prayed for said he felt a lot better. The next day at work he told me that he picked up his son that morning (who is around 2-3 years old) because he 'forgot' his back was sore. A few days later he told me that he actually felt his spine realigning when I prayed. Yesterday he told me he had cancelled his next chiropractor appointment! Praise God :)

Perfect baby...

In early February I had the opportunity to meet and pray for a woman called M. She was about 6 months pregnant at the time. I prayed for her and the baby, that all would be well for the baby and for the Mum, not really knowing anything about her background or circumstances, etc .

Later into the pregnancy, I found out that the baby was diagnosed as having Down Syndrome and was missing a nose. I was told that the mother of this baby was in shock and in total fear of how she was going to cope with such a baby.

Some time later, at church, I heard a testimony of a woman in our church praying for a pregnant woman who had also been told that she was carrying a baby with Downs Syndrome. The woman at church had prayed for the pregnant woman and the baby had been completely healed by God. When I heard the testimony at church I elbowed my husband and said, "that's for M" and I 'took' the testimony for her, knowing what God had done for one   he could and would do for her   and so, when I saw M again, I was full of faith and I released the testimony and God's Kingdom over her, praying for the same a fully healthy baby...

On the way to church last Sunday (May 5) I heard the news that the baby had been born at home, early that morning, and that the baby appeared to be totally healthy, with a fully formed nose.

I was told that, after getting to the hospital, the doctors assessed the baby, in full knowledge of the diagnosis of Down Syndrome and that although all appeared well, a blood test would have to be done to be sure the baby was fully healthy.

Late Monday afternoon, the blood tests came back... all clear!

I saw the baby today. He is totally healed, totally whole, and is absolutely delightful!!!!!

Glory to God!!!

The priority of heaven is the presence of the King. The priority of heaven is devotion to God, worship of God, intimacy with God and affection for God. Disciples who make this their priority understand that they can move beyond the notion that God visits us, to the reality that God wants to co-habit with us all the time. Jesus' model for life was to be absorbed and immersed in God. Jesus prayer in Mark 14:36 reveals much about His relationship with God:

> *And He was saying, "Abba! Father! All things are possible for You; remove this cup from Me; yet not what I will, but what You will."*

His relationship was personal – 'Abba! Father!' He believed the Father was the resource for life – 'all things are possible for You;' He was totally yielded and dependent – 'yet not what I will, but what You will.' He expressed hope and trust in adversity.

We can see the importance of valuing God's presence in Moses' declaration:

> *Then he said to Him, "If Your presence does not go with us, do not lead us up from here. For how then can it be known that I have found favor in Your sight, I and Your people? Is it not by Your going with us, so that we, I and Your people, may be distinguished from all the other people who are upon the face of the earth?"* (Exodus 33:15 & 16)

The significance of His presence is found in contrasting the way Jonah and Jesus managed the storms they found themselves in (Jonah 1 and 2 / Matthew 8:23–27). Jonah was asleep in his boat in the midst of a storm because he was depressed. Jesus was asleep in his boat in the midst of a storm because He was at peace. Jonah cried out to God in prayer beseeching God to intervene. Jesus prayed with faith because of a promise, addressing the problem situation with authority.

The disciples prayed like Jonah – *wake up Jesus; don't you care about our predicament?* Jesus did not take on their fear and responded by binding and rebuking the storm. Jesus lived in peace and God's presence and so released what He lived in. Peace is not the absence of conflict; it is the presence of a person. Peace subdues. (Philippians 5:7) As we are citizens of heaven (Philippians 3:20) we can live in this world with another world's reality and authority. We are to represent that world.

Jonah's storm was to drive him back to the will of God. Jesus' storm was to release the disciples into who they were. Jesus wanted them to see that we are to deal with obstacles to the will of God by being aware of His presence and acting on in the authority we have. Do what the occasion demands and allow the mystery of Christ within to be expressed.

We see God responding to Moses in a similar way:

But Moses said to the people, "Do not fear! Stand by and see the salvation of the LORD which He will accomplish for you today; for the Egyptians whom you have seen today, you will never see them again forever. The LORD will fight for you while you keep silent."

Then the LORD said to Moses, "Why are you crying out to Me? Tell the sons of Israel to go forward. As for you, lift up your staff and stretch out your hand over the sea and divide it, and the sons of Israel shall go through the midst of the sea on dry land. As for Me, behold, I will harden the hearts of the Egyptians so that they will go in after them; and I will be honored through Pharaoh and all his army, through his chariots and his horsemen. Then the Egyptians will know that I am the LORD, when I am honored through Pharaoh, through his chariots and his horsemen." (Exodus 14:13–18)

God couldn't move until Moses exercised His authority. God says – why are you crying out to Me? Use what I have given you, what's in your hand; use your authority. Most Christians live with a concept that the normal Christian life is for God to invade the earth but He wants us to be his invasion of the earth. We are called to release heaven on earth, like Jesus did.

Jonah's boat was going to be shipwrecked unless there was repentance. Jesus' boat was going to be shipwrecked unless there was faith. As we maintain a priority of intimacy that values presence, we will discover that we are more aware of His reality that than the world's reality. From this position we are able to discover faith and be like Jesus in every way.

Our standing with God has been restored (1 Corinthians 1:9). We are loved as sons. In fact, we are loved just as much as Jesus.

I in them and You in Me, that they may be perfected in unity, so that the world may know that You sent Me, and loved them, even as You have loved Me. (John 17:23)

We grow in the knowledge of what sonship means; we do not grow in sonship. The more we realise who we are in Christ, the more we love who we really are.

WHAT INHERITANCE HAVE WE RECEIVED?

We have received an extraordinary inheritance.

Colossians 1:12 lays it out clearly:

giving thanks to the Father, who has qualified us to share in the inheritance of the saints in Light.

God qualifies the called, He does not call the qualified. His focus is not on our adequacy, it is on our availability. We walk in our inheritance on the basis of being and becoming, not performance and behaviour.

Further, 1 Corinthians 2:12 assures us:

Now we have received, not the spirit of the world, but the Spirit who is from God, so that we may know the things freely given to us by God,

We have received much more than a 'get out of jail free' card. An inheritance ignored is an opportunity lost. An inheritance invested has the capacity to influence generations.

- Our inheritance in Jesus consists of so much including:
- to have perfect fellowship with the Father;
- to be a son of God;
- to be righteous;
- to have all authority;
- to release the government of God into the earth;
- to have the Spirit in us;
- to have the Spirit on us for the demonstration of the power of God;
- to stand in the presence of God without guilt or inferiority; and,
- to be free from all claims of justice against us as they have been satisfied.

The truth is that we already have all we need to do the works that Jesus did –and even greater works (John 14:12). As Jesus has gone to the Father we have every spiritual blessing on heaven and in earth (Ephesians 1:3); we are divine in nature (2 Peter 1:1–10); the kingdom is within us (Luke 17:21); and rivers of living water flow out of us (John 7:38). The question now is how to release what is already in us.

The key to release is **agreement**. Agreeing with what God says about us and our circumstances, **not** agreeing with our own understanding. Faith and belief are our places of agreement and are discovered through repentance. That is, changing the way we think to believe in the gospel of the Kingdom. We need to step out of the way this world thinks and step into the way that God thinks (1 Corinthians 2).

As we embrace our identity, be passionate in our intimacy (friendship) and invest our inheritance, we position ourselves to have extraordinary influence to expand and fill the earth with His kingdom.

I was thrown off a horse when I was eight years old. I know how powerful they are. If they realised their power, they could dominate us. Disciples who know they can be like Jesus in every way can dominate all the other influences that harm the pinnacle of God's creation – human beings.

Jesus was bold in declaring:

'If I do not do the works of My Father, do not believe Me.' (John 10:37)

What a difference it makes to our view of the normal Christian life if we take this on as the qualification for discipleship. Paul longed for his influence to increase and identified living from the knowledge of his imputed righteousness as a key.

More than that, I count all things to be loss in view of the surpassing value of knowing Christ Jesus my Lord, for whom I have suffered the loss of all things, and count them but rubbish so that I may gain Christ, and may be found in Him, not having a righteousness of my own derived from the Law, but that which is through faith in Christ, the righteousness which comes from God on the basis of faith, that I may know Him and the power of His resurrection and the fellowship of His sufferings, being conformed to His death; in order that I may attain to the resurrection from the dead. (Philippians 3:8–11)

God has anointed us according to how He sees us, not according to how we see ourselves. His fullness is in us. His ability is in us. His resources are at our disposal. His love nature dwells within us. Faith working though love changes the natural world. As we learn to walk in a manner worthy of the Lord (Colossians 1:10) so do we:

- reign in life not through what we do but through what we receive;
- receive abundant grace through the gift of righteousness;
- can invade the impossible because everything is already under Jesus' feet;
- know we are righteous in God's eyes all the time as a gift and His glory does not have to fade;
- rejoice in the knowledge that the Holy Spirit came upon Jesus as a man not as God. We too can do the works He did as the Holy Spirit will empower us in the same way and,
- seize the initiative from the hands of the devil.

As a result, the vision of Stairway Church – what we *see* – is people who:

- are intimate with God and others;
- live from their identity in Christ;
- use their inheritance in Christ to advance His kingdom;.
- partner with God to influence their world, the church and generations;
- together host the manifest presence of God.

Our mission – why we *exist* – is:
- responding to God's heart so His presence and power are expressed in our world.

Chapter Four
COLLECTIVE EFFORT

As I look back to those days I am inclined to believe that the type of life I led at home, my experience in the Veld where we worked and played together in groups, introduced me at an early age to the ideas of collective effort. The little progress I made in this regard was undermined by the type of formal education I received, which tended to stress individuality more than collective values.

– Nelson Mandela –

There is an old saying that it takes a village to raise a child. Galatians 4:19 reads:

My children, with whom I am again in labor until Christ is formed in you—

The process and challenge of becoming and making disciples requires a unified approach. There is greater power when we are learning together to acknowledge who we have already become as new creations. The strength and power of collective effort propels us ever faster towards a higher place in the Spirit. When people stand together in unity and love the miracle realm is easy to enter.

We need the support and encouragement of others to go on a journey into glory and intimacy. The normal Christian life is to demonstrate who God is, to demonstrate what God is like, to destroy the work of the devil, and to be a part of transforming the planet into a place that is radiant and saturated with His power and presence. To do this and to be like Jesus in every way we need to learn how to look at life, its circumstances and everything we experience from heaven's perspective. However, other perspectives have been formed in us that compete for dominance in our hearts and thought life.

Only a renewed mind can constantly bring kingdom activity to the earth. Renewing the mind begins with repentance; that is, going back to God's perspective on reality. Most Christians have repented enough to be forgiven, but not enough to see the kingdom by both declaring the kingdom is at hand *and* demonstrating its effects. This is a challenging journey that can only successfully be taken in community.

As a community of faith at Stairway Church we have travelled away from being satisfied with just a church experience. We have embraced being co-labourers with Jesus in a clash of two kingdoms. We believe in the kingdom being released on earth now and we are therefore called to invade the impossible. Our priorities are to impact the spirit world with the overwhelming victory of the cross and to manage our spirituality so that we become who we already are.

Our foundation is that God is good. Our framework is that nothing is impossible. Our focus is that Jesus has won the victory. Our fruit is disciples that are releasing heaven on earth. These shared values are the context for our engagement as a community of faith in making disciples.

I asked our congregation this question: *As you have changed your view of the normal Christian life, how important has it been to be supported by our community life together?* Here are some of their responses:

Identity found...

Several years ago, I looked at myself in the mirror one morning and didn't recognise me. It was very odd, uncomfortable and a bit scary to suddenly not know the person I had become.

I knew instantly it was a God thing and thinking of that time now, I'd say I'd been pushing against something for a long time and had suddenly broken through.

Over the next weeks I realised that everything I did had changed. Thought processes I had held for fifty-plus years had changed. I freaked but chose to partner with and trust my Dad (Father God) in fully becoming who I was always meant to be. It took twelve to eighteen months to work through this process of becoming comfortable in my new skin.

Now, on the other side of all that was, life is amazing. I know who I am! I know my identity and live out of that. I know my God is a God of healing and freedom and heaven can and does invade earth through me.

Essential encouragement...

The Sunday services are crucial for my encouragement. They give me courage. I hear every week at least one testimony of how God has worked. This enlarges my experience of God and how He works, and it gives me courage to go and do the same. I can relate to the different feelings of inadequacy, etc. and it gives me courage.

Inseparable encounter and community...

I cannot begin to fully express how amazing it has been to be a part of a community of faith who together are intentionally pressing into the revelation that it is indeed our portion to do and see 'the greater works than these', that Jesus spoke of when he walked the earth. I am so thankful for our weekend gatherings, connect groups etc., that have supported me and my family in sustaining a passion for more of Jesus and inspiration and motivation to see heaven coming to earth through our lives in everyday situations. There is a phrase that God has been unpacking for me over the past couple of months that explains more clearly how important our gathering are on this journey of exploring the parameters of the 'normal Christian life'. It's all about ENCOUNTER AND COMMUNITY! The two together in partnership, you can't have one without the other!

Confidence to keep learning and growing...

Confidence is a very big key in my world and being connected to other people who are on the same journey helps me keep a focus on the Kingdom. It's so easy for me to get caught up in the grind of daily life and, in that, to become completely earthbound in my thinking. Hearing the ongoing testimonies through weekend services and making it a habit to connect through Stairway College has really helped me. Also I have realised more fully that His gifting in me is so often tied up to His complete body. How well I go as an individual is inextricably connected to how well I'm connected to his body and without a human connection I reckon I could get off on a tangent and miss both His fullness in my life and my full contribution to His community.

Attending Stairway and going to the College has transformed my life and at 59 I have learned 'you can teach aging dogs new tricks'. Before starting College I thought I did not hear from God or not very often. I started with Experiencing the Presence of the Spirit. I was not getting anything when others were feeling the presence till week four when we were doing supernatural worship and I got a few pictures that I doodled and found they were exactly the same pictures Ursula had received. I had break through that night. In the following weeks I started to get praying in tongues which was something I had been praying for, for several years. During this course I received a lot of personal healing around spiritual abuse and a number of other issues and God just turned my life around. It led to changes in employment and a greater faith in God's ability to show up for me and how much He loved me.

I also learned that I carried a presence with me as when I returned to a previous employer that the end of last year they welcomed me back, which I felt good about and when I thanked the EO for his kind words he said you reap what you sow and you sowed well last time (which I had not been conscious about).

As I have continued to undertake more College courses, attend conferences and regular services, I have continued to be overwhelmed by God's goodness and our ability to carry that into our daily situations and bring Heaven to earth for those around us.

The above are just small examples of the way my life has changed in the last few years. I have started to document a lot of the things that have happened, as God's favour on me and my family is just amazing.

At this point it will be helpful to revisit some of my previously published words in *Above the Line* about disciple making.

Jesus taught his disciples to pray on earth as it is in Heaven (Matthew 6:10). Jesus has sent us into the world as the Father sent Him (John 20:21). This is why Jesus could confidently declare that we would at least do the same works that He did (John 14:12).

Sadly, this is not the reality of many 21st century Western Christians. Our congregations are on the whole, well managed. Some congregations are led by charismatic, highly-gifted and strongly motivated leaders who are accomplishing some incredible things. However, honesty demands that we ask whether much of Heaven is reaching earth through our congregations. There is clearly room for far greater manifestations of healing, deliverance, salvation, miracles and acts of redemptive power. We have discovered sound order but are all things being done? (1 Corinthians 14:40) Is Jesus receiving His full reward for the price He paid on the cross?

When Jesus left the earth His vision was that we would make disciples and be made into disciples (Matthew 28:18–20). Disciples that would walk on the earth in the same manner that Jesus walked (1 John 2:6). Jesus said that He would build His church (Matthew 18:18) and He asked us to make disciples.

In life when we make something we follow directions or a plan to achieve a specific outcome. If our aim is to make a chair we will not be satisfied if we produce a table. We know what a chair looks like and the purpose it serves. Making disciples should be the same. I wonder, though, if churches and their leaders have thought about the disciples they are making. What will they look like? How will they think? Feel? Clearly much thought goes into what programmes will look like, and their desired outcome. But in the end, what is being created?

Our discovery of pursuing a life together 'above the line' has resulted in a picture of disciples who have four characteristics. First, a disciple of Jesus is on the way to learning self-governance. Central to the Christian faith is the notion of free will. I need to repent of my sins because I have *chosen* to act in a way that opposes God. No one compelled me to sin. I chose to do so; therefore I am personally responsible. To be self-governing means to be self-aware and to take personal responsibility for my attitudes, actions and thoughts. Jesus identified this reality when He said that it was not what goes into the heart of a man that defiles him but what comes out of the heart (Mark 7:14–23). Disciples of Jesus are called to be self-governing because they love their life and do not want to lose it.

Second, disciples of Jesus are in the process of learning to be innately powerful. That is, their relationship is directly moulded and influenced by determining to grow the fruit of the Spirit (Galatians 5:22–23). Disciples should aspire to treat everyone in their lives with love, joy, peace, patience, kindness, goodness, faithfulness, gentleness and self-control. Through self-awareness they will find they can recognise when others' motives and attitudes are having an impact on their relationships. Through personal responsibility, they repent and ask for grace to bring the fruit of the Spirit to live in their heart. Once the fruit of the Spirit is growing there, they learn not to return to their own ways of treating people, but to be innately powerful in maintaining relationships on the basis of the fruit of the Spirit. Disciples of Jesus are called to be innately powerful because they are discovering how to choose to love others.

Third, disciples of Jesus will learn to be inherently supernatural. That is, they will want to do the works that Jesus did because they know *who they are* in Christ. They are convinced that the same Holy Spirit who raised Jesus from the dead abides in them. Consequently, they both believe in and look for opportunities to release the power and presence of Jesus in their daily lives. These disciples believe in 'Heaven on earth' released through them because Jesus said this would be so (John 14:12). Disciples of Jesus are called to be inherently supernatural because it is a characteristic of those who love God.

Fourth, disciples of Jesus will build significant lifestyles in Christ as they love God (be inherently supernatural), love others (be innately powerful) and love themselves (be self governing). In that order. As the two great commandments are pursued, everything else will fall into place (Matthew 22:40). That is, a significant lifestyle in Christ will emerge for the disciples as they are involved in advancing the kingdom of God on the earth. To sum up, disciples of Jesus will build significant lifestyles that advance the kingdom as they love God, others and self.

The territory that accompanies leadership is exhilarating and demanding; pleasurable and painful; releasing and responsible; and, breathtaking in breakthrough and overwhelming in opportunities. Leaders are gatekeepers. The influence they exercise is at once extraordinary... and humbling. Church leaders, whether paid or unpaid, senior or junior, on their own or in a team, are stewards of a vision that has its origins in the heart of God.

Leaders are catalysts for change and new growth. What happens in a leader, through encounters with God, can shape and form the things of Heaven in those they influence. If the churches we lead are not producing and developing battle ready disciples who are self-governing, innately powerful, inherently 'supernatural' and with significant lifestyles in Christ, then why not? Are we so focussed below the line that we are simply managing people in different seasons of their lives and giving them something to do?

Martha was managing an event that Jesus had not asked for. (Luke 10:38-42) Her hospitality and zeal are to be commended as worthwhile and impressive. However, she was so focussed on achievement she lost sight of affection. Instead she was worried and bothered. Martha was looking to the appropriateness of principles with the result that the presence of Jesus (and Mary) was minimised. Martha became demanding, turning to matters of the 'wineskin' with the result the she was 'distracted with all her preparations'. Her below the line emphasis resulted in attitudes and behaviours that are all-too-familiar to church leaders and their congregations. On the other hand, Mary chose the good part, the one thing that is necessary. She was focussed on affection, presence and the 'wine'.

With these outcomes in mind we have taken collective responsibility to be a disciple-making community that is shaped by creating atmospheres to experience and encounter God. To do this we have focused attention and energy into: our adoration of God; being contributors; growing in the fruit of the Spirit; cultivating a desire to know and be known deeply; being humble; and, giving honour.

Adoration of God is based on the belief that God is good. It results in a heart-felt desire to know what God is saying about the relationships and circumstances that are in my life and joining myself to what He is saying. Adoration acknowledges that it is because of Him I live this way. For example, judging others with mercy; putting to death the fruit of the flesh; doing as much good as I can; releasing heaven on earth etc. Adoration is the motivation for my spiritual life. As a consequence I am not focussed on spiritual disciplines as much as I express spiritual desires.

Being contributors results in us gathering together around who Jesus is. It promotes a desire to share our experiences, both positive and negative. It fosters a need to pray together and for one another. It results in us having testimonies of what God is doing that we want to relate to one another.

Growing in the fruit of the Spirit is a place of both self awareness and being accountable. It values character development, honesty and a dependence on one another. It is recognition that love is the greatest of all (1 Corinthians 13). Growing in the fruit of the Spirit captures the development of key attributes of the nature and character of God. It results in deliverance and the healing of past wounds. If we stay in the fruit of the Spirit the devil has nothing to engage with.

Cultivating a desire to know and be known by others is the core value of heart to heart relationships. It is the place of discovering another's hopes and dreams so that we can help those be realised. Being known includes allowing others to see who I really am under pressure knowing I will be accepted yet challenged to move beyond my current limitations. It allows for father/son and mother/daughter relationships to be fostered as a means of being family and achieving generational impact.

Being humble is the key to taking personal responsibility. It allows the emergence of a government of love where protecting relationships that bring freedom are possible. With humility we learn to manage ourselves to protect relationships rather than control others through rules. Being humble is the foundation on which we teach and lead, through example, how to be like Jesus (Philippians 2:5–11).

Giving honour results in a focus on another's gift and call, not our position and power. Honouring the apostle as much as the one who serves through cleaning the bathrooms because position and power are no longer relevant. Elevating the status of everyone because their gift and call are from God. When we honour them we honour the gift giver. Giving glory to and promote all: 'as they are dearly loved by God so they are dearly loved by me'. Respecting and admiring people, being determined to not disempower or control them.

There is so much more to say here. In the next chapter I will group adoration of God, being a contributor and growing in the Spirit together, to look at how to grow and develop the *Spirit Life* of a community of faith that fosters the making of disciples who will be like Jesus in every way. Similarly, the subsequent chapter will group cultivating a desire to know and be known deeply, being humble and giving honour together, to look at how to grow and develop the style of *Community Life* that fosters the making of disciples who will be like Jesus in every way.

I asked our congregation – *In comparison to your understanding of the normal Christian life, describe the most significant changes in yourself as you have embraced the truth that you have been giving the right to be like Jesus in every way.* Here are some of their responses:

Fear gone...

First of all the 'fear of man' has been 'broken off' my life. I am growing in the relationships I do have, instead of being isolated, and so becoming more confident in my daily life. The concept of being able to walk in 'dominion' in my daily life is growing as I embrace being like Jesus and I am not as easily intimidated as before. My confidence and faith in my prayers being heard has increased amazingly. When I do experience a discouraging time I am able to bounce back in my faith but also to let people speak into my life, which helps. I am no longer being isolated by fear and if fear comes then I know it can and will be dealt with. I cannot thank the leadership of Stairway Church enough for the courage they have taken to allow us all to be free to be who God created us to be.

Healing without a licence...

I love that God can heal the sick through me. I may just be Dr. Helen (as my parents hoped I would be) after all. The big difference is I am a faithful servant to God and I don't really have to do anything but give people a God encounter and God heals people through me. The life of a Christian is far more fun than I could have ever imagined.

Fuelled up and ready to go...

I now know I carry the same compassion, grace and healing power that Jesus displayed in the bible. I don't need to ask God for more power, I have been given everything I need when I received Christ and the Holy Spirit to carry love, grace and healing to others when they need it and personally, no matter what life brings.

Walking in my purpose and identity...

Over the years and thanks to the transformations God performed in my life, He brought to my attention how to act in certain situations and towards others. I had to ask myself 'what would Jesus do/say?' I had to search for the answers by looking at the character of Jesus. It changed my life and my heart towards others completely. From then on I felt how He was at work all the time through me to impact others without me even noticing it was happening. Someone said to me once 'I don't know why but when I see you I just can't stop talking' (usually about a hurt they had). It made me realise that I was learning from Him and in doing that becoming in some way like him.

Then things started to fall in place as I was becoming able to carry out His purposes. It wasn't complicated; all I had to do was listen to people, usually women and many times singles who needed to be shown kindness and be listened to. This was happening well before I received a prophecy which was exactly about that, and it confirms His purpose was at work in my life. To arrive to this I had to learn to know what Jesus would do in my situation and had to learn to be more like Him and show the love and kindness He would have for others even when it was hard.

I know what love is...

An understanding of 'love' as it is meant to be would have to be the most significant change for me in grabbing hold of who Jesus really is and stepping into and being more like who He is.

A couple of years ago I started saying, 'I have no idea what love is.' I knew God is love. I'd learned that in Sunday school a long time ago but my idea of love, through experience, was incredibly warped and so my idea of God's love was also warped.

Over time, He has loved me and taught me to love myself and others. I am still a work in progress.

Love is who He is! Every good thing flows out of heaven in love, His pure love.

A change of focus...

I think the most significant change for me as I have embraced the truth about being given the right to be like Jesus is the simplicity. It's taken away the tension. I used to think how am I going to do this? Will I embarrass myself? What if I stuff up? I realized that I was still thinking of my own issues and not having enough compassion for the other person. I was too self-focused.

When I realised that I needed to focus toward others I went to God for help. I asked Him for guidance and patience to take my hand and lead me, not once but consistently over and over and as I explained to God that I felt my imperfectness would fail me and that I would need His help through this transitional stage, realising that I would still need to petition God indefinitely.

Chapter Five
SPIRIT LIFE

Be preoccupied with Jesus, then intimacy will always defeat intimidation.

– Graham Cooke –

Jesus wants us to be absorbed and immersed in God as He was.

But when the fullness of the time came, God sent forth His Son, born of a woman, born under the Law, so that He might redeem those who were under the Law, that we might receive the adoption as sons. Because you are sons, God has sent forth the Spirit of His Son into our hearts, crying, "Abba! Father!" Therefore you are no longer a slave, but a son; and if a son, then an heir through God (Galatians 4:4–7).

Jesus was devoted to finding and doing the will of the Father. Jesus was in complete union with the Father through the Spirit – not just for a period of time or for a particular task as is found in the Old Testament. We are called to live this way. In any situation we find ourselves in, we are to learn to look for what God might be trying to do and join ourselves to that. This is easier said than done! In community we can learn from one another's experience. We have found that a culture where 'every attempt is a success' helps break down the power of fear and failure.

Jesus fulfilled his mission through being immersed in the person and grace of the Holy Spirit. John 20 records the following:

So when it was evening on that day, the first day of the week, and when the doors were shut where the disciples were, for fear of the Jews, Jesus came and stood in their midst and said to them, "Peace be with you." And when He had said this, He showed them both His hands and His side. The disciples then rejoiced when they saw the Lord. So Jesus said to them again, "Peace be with you; as the Father has sent Me, I also send you." And when He had said this, He breathed on them and said to them, "Receive the Holy Spirit.

As Jesus sent His disciples to do what He had done, He wanted them to be in the person and grace of the Holy Spirit. They were then also to wait in Jerusalem for the Holy Spirit because it was the only way they would know what God was doing. It was an experience they were to have together. It was the Holy Spirit who would make them witnesses.

Is it possible that in all our zeal and motivation to be witnesses that we have turned to man-made programmes, thus turning God's initiative into human enterprise? When we in community host the presence of the Holy Spirit, His life is poured into us and we have faith to be like Jesus in our daily lives.

An aspect of our growing commitment to releasing the Kingdom in our daily lives has been to embrace an idea known as 'Treasure Hunts'. People gather together in prayer and worship in order to seek from the Holy Spirit clues about their 'treasure' (usually people at local shopping complexes). Clues include identifiable features like clothing or physical appearance. They then travel to the shopping centre and go out in pairs to look for the 'treasure' God has identified for them to bless. They then approach their treasure and offer to be a blessing. Here are some of their stories:

A first time treasure hunter shares their experience at a local shopping centre...

I finally came across a man with his arm in a sling in the fruit and veggie area. We slipped easily into a conversation about his arm and I found out that he had had an accident with a chain saw (not exactly an elbow problem, which was the word I felt God give me). I must admit I felt nervous; however I really wanted to pray for him for a reduction of pain.

When I asked him if I could pray, he and his wife declined, assuring me that he had a good physician looking after him. Initially I felt disappointed, but I was encouraged that every attempt is a success. I am looking forward to going out next time to hunt for more 'treasures' and most importantly to release the goodness of God.

A treasure hunter training other treasure hunters...

Last weekend we went to a shopping centre and felt God lead us to speak with a woman who was doing her grocery shopping. So I grabbed a 'first-timer' and we approached her. As we began speaking to her I felt to ask if she had any pain in her back. It turns out that she had recently had four compression fractures in her spine and was in pain. She was also worried about developing a hunch back, so we asked if we could pray. Then God showed up and she was healed. No more pain and she was able to stand up straight. Then she tells us that she also suffers from depression and asked if we could pray for that too, which my colleague did. She was thrilled and we were stoked to have seen God move in this lady's life in the way He had.

A second time treasure hunter moves from task to releasing God's love to people...

So, we were experimenting in hearing God's voice to find 'treasures' to pray for. As we walked around looking for our 'treasures', the Holy Spirit was reminding me about releasing the goodness of God rather than being task oriented. I used to feel like 'I must get someone saved, I must pray for someone... etc'. My journey in evangelism has been moving from task orientation, towards living a life that releases God's affection and goodness to people. It is still a journey, standing against the nerves that compete against that sense of affection and goodness of God. Amazing things can happen though when love is released. God really is good and has nice things to say to people.

Age doesn't matter – a first time experience for a child...

Last Saturday we went out to a local shopping centre to do some outreach with the Spirit-led Evangelism Team. The youngest team member that day was only five, but she wasn't going to let that slow her down. As we were standing around getting our bearings and starting to look for the treasures on our lists, this little five-year-old saw a family walk past and the child was coughing. So she grabbed her dad and went after them so she could pray for the child. They turned down the offer, but she seemed to just brush it off and move on. Her dad had a word for a lady with a pink top, white hair and carpal tunnel. They found a lady (the third attempt) who it turns out had carpal tunnel and the pain went all the way up her arm. As they asked her she seemed quite surprised that they would know this about her, and gratefully accepted the offer of this child to pray. When they had finished the lady said it felt much better. Later on the child's dad asked her what that was like and said she could feel the lady's arm shaking as she prayed.

I watched a few times, then I took the plunge...

It was my first time seeing anything like this. I was taught that Evangelism was only for the gifted people and I should just invite people to church to hear the visiting preacher. I watched others stepping out and saw how excited they were, even when people turned them down. Then I felt God lead me towards someone, so I took a deep breath, swallowed my fear and approached them. I realized after I starting speaking that I had no idea what to say, so I stumbled over my words and nothing came out right. They were polite, but not interested. But I had stepped up and I felt God smile at me and say, 'well done, son'.

After a year of being too scared she took the first step...

It took a year to build up the courage to go on her first treasure hunt, and when she got there she was both nervous and excited. As we prayed, she felt God leading her to buy flowers. She thought she would buy them and give them away to bless people. When she got to the shopping centre she felt to buy individually wrapped gerberas, but the florist didn't have any, so she asked if a couple of bunches could be individually wrapped. This took some time, which at first was frustrating, until the florist started to ask questions and it became apparent that she was the treasure that God had led her to.

In our life as a community we endeavour to model our mission each day on the recognition of what the Spirit may be doing in our circumstances and relationships, and dedicate ourselves to that. This has resulted in a growing commitment to follow the Spirit's 'un-guessable' options. The alternative to this open choice that enables discernment is to return to a code of regulations that maintains unnecessary safety. The Holy Spirit is not bound, and like the wind we are not to be restricted by obligation or convention when His presence comes and His power is released. On this basis, we corporately allow moments of heightened spiritual awareness to unfold to discover God in the midst of them. Mistakes are made, but more often the Spirit comes in power and opens eyes that are closed, opens hearts that are unaware and opens minds that have shrunk from too much reality.

Jesus had times of self-surrender that defied logic and cultural conventions – spitting in dirt, and then rubbing the resultant clay in the eyes of a blind man to release the miracle of sight; spitting on a mute man's tongue to release the gift of speech; instructing unclean lepers to present themselves to the priest for healing; turning water into wine; walking on water; finding money in the mouth of a fish. There is a love for God and others that requires us to step away from self-interest and make sacrifices for the sake of others. This is how the Spirit can lead. We learn in community, through story-telling and from each other's exploits, to take our own risks.

We are created to trust God and to run the risks of life in the Spirit. To trust the Spirit's unpredictable responses. We can only be powerful transmitting stations of God's reality if we have become powerful receivers. To do this we need to be more focused on hearing God's voice than responding to the human voices of fear and doubt. Our whole lives need to become a response to the call of God. We grow in confidence that we are hearing from the Lord when we practise in safe environments. So we build a community that fosters mutual respect and encouragement in demonstrating how to hear from God and act on it.

We are to learn *with* one another, *through* one another and *for* one another.

I asked our staff the following: *As a key leader in our community of faith, what have been your greatest joys and challenges in helping our congregation change their understanding of the normal Christian life?*

Here are some of their responses:

Neil Dowling

The greatest joy for me in the last five to seven years has been seeing people take extraordinary risks with their faith. In the beginning of our journey we seemed to have very few testimonies of people who were prepared to step out of their particular boat into the unchartered water of walking with God wherever He was walking!

Over the past few years we have seen an ever-increasing flow of God stories telling of people partnering with God in their everyday lives. Whether that is in shopping mall, work situations or check-out lines, average people in our church are finding that being bold in faith causes fascinating encounters in all sorts of situations. One of the great encouragements in this development has been the maxim spoken from the pulpit, namely, **'that every attempt is a success!'** As a staff, we have probably given equal place to those who are **'just having a go'** as we have to those whose stories were spectacularly successful. Today it seems normal Christianity that no church meeting is complete without a number of 'now' God stories being unwrapped at the same time.

I think that the challenge for our church in the journey has been to **'normalize'** the gifts that God has given for the building of the church as spoken in I Corinthians 12. While we have always believed and practised the gifts of the Holy Spirit, more often than not this was practised from the safety of the inner sanctum, rather than being taken out into our community. Our College has played a major role in helping large numbers of our church congregation become familiar and practised as God's Spirit became our friend and not just our tutor! How amazing to find ourselves looking for God's leading in the 'normal' as heaven comes to earth!!

Julie Sgarlata

My greatest joy has been to see people changing their mindset about their identity. I have watched as many members of our congregation continue to develop an intimate relationship with God, hear His voice and move out with confidence. An appreciation that we are all made 'in God's image' teaches us that we **all** have gold deposited within us, so we begin to look for what's right in each other instead of looking for what's wrong. A congregation of radical, passionate lovers of God will lay down their lives in obedience, being sensitive to His Spirit. A people who live for God will do whatever it takes to pursue more of His presence. We are becoming a people of His presence who are learning to change the atmosphere and effect the environment in which we live. We are creating the conditions for which we attract the things of heaven – so that heaven can invade the earth!

Ursula Cettolin

As a worship leader I knew how to direct people through the singing time.

So when Peter started to talk specifically to the worship team about hosting God's Presence together, I was not entirely sure what that looked like. Weren't we already doing that? At the same time, as a church, we were going on a journey to discover what it truly meant to live as children of God. As we began to take on this mindset we began to ask questions: Why did we sing as though He was not in the room? Were we really expectant that our loving Heavenly Father would speak and act in our services? Why did we not really allow Holy Spirit to lead – or at least it sometimes seemed like that amidst the need to get through our five practiced arrangements of songs in the twenty five minute slot!

There was no fail proof formula for the kind of 'walking off the map' that the answers to these questions required. So it was vital that the pursuit of His Presence and our growth in identity as His much loved children went hand in hand. As worship leaders we not only needed to grow in our experience of God's Presence in worship – but we also needed to grow together with the congregation. We did not want to be a worship team off on our own musical trip, leaving everyone else to find their own way! The challenge lay before all of us to carve out this new path of Hosting His Presence!

Worship is actually a spiritual tool God has given His children to see the Kingdom of heaven invade earth. We knew it as a nice concept, but probably not the breadth of its reality. Our congregation has now taken hold of this and recognise that worship is not just a nice sing along together.

We're actually opening up an atmosphere for God encounters. Our worship is bigger than just the room! Children of God know their authority.

The great thing is that people are living, aware of hosting His Presence all throughout their weeks. They are seeking His face and carrying the sense of Him wanting to act and speak in their everyday lives. They are endeavouring to have a Mary heart (sitting at the feet of Jesus) first and foremost. They are walking into each day knowing they are loved children of God. So when we gather together to worship, it can't help but become this explosion of all God is doing and saying and revealing. It becomes this unstoppable passion that just keeps building! Sometimes it's still building long after the worship team are ready to call it a day! As worship leaders we could never with our cleverest ways and most loving prayers ignite this passion in people like the Holy Spirit has. He makes us look pretty good as a worship team!

What we are seeing now is that it is more and more the norm that the congregation are the ones directing the worship and the worship team being facilitators. The result has been His manifest Presence, seen in healing, visions, breakthroughs, miracles, signs and wonders. Heaven invading earth! I look around Stairway in our gatherings and it looks like people worshipping with their whole heart, soul, mind and body (Luke 10:27). It's rarely predictable in nature, but always passionate in pursuit of His Presence. It looks like a bunch of joyful children running headlong into the arms of their loving Father. Yeah, it looks a lot like a 'free church' to me. We can never go back!

Roselyn Owen

As the Children's Pastor at Stairway one of the challenges I faced was to remove the myth of leadership that people can't go where I haven't been myself. I think this is a false ceiling that I've been able to see Jesus lift off. Jesus is the good shepherd who wants to lead and speak to his children; my role is as the gatekeeper who opens the gate and is caretaker, but

Jesus Himself does the leading, the speaking and teaching. It is the same resurrected Jesus who walked alongside the disciples who wants to open up the scriptures to us, especially children! He said to 'learn from Me'; I've found that to be more literal than we thought... He is still the teacher and good shepherd. He will reveal things supernaturally/naturally to children. The great joy in this for me and our volunteer leadership team is we've learned to be gatekeepers and to host the presence of God, it is Jesus who does most of the leading in a child's life.

As the gatekeeper, I open the gate, He does come in. He always wants to lead and guide, to touch his children in sometimes astonishing ways. We teach children He always has something to 'show, tell or give' them. My part is helping children discover the ways that Jesus does just that. It is also a two way learning. I listen to the children and learn how Jesus is revealing himself to them and teaching them personally.

Following are some stories of Jesus leading and guiding our children:

Single mum of three young children...

I really wanted to go to church again tonight and take the kids (something I've never done on my own, i.e go to church at night with the kids) So I floated the idea past the kids and they were happy enough to go. I think it was a God thing as they were pretty tired from the weekend, and even I wondered if it was a good idea! We sat down near the front for worship, but I didn't feel the presence of God too much, even though many others were. Partly though, I think it was because I had to keep an eye on what the kids were doing.

The kids ended up getting a bit too restless, so I took them into the mothers' room, and there was no one else in there but us. Then there was a shift in the worship when Derek and Lucy Bailey started leading it. It was amazing and the presence of God was very powerful. I had my hands raised in worship (Grace had been playing on the floor). She came over to me and put her hands in my hands. I asked her if she could feel the presence of

God. She said yes, so I started to pray for her, to talk to her, I asked her what she could feel and then it went from there.

She said she felt like raindrops of love falling down. I asked her if they were warm or cool, and she said 'just right'. Then she said she felt like God had given her a key to heaven and an angel was leading her to Jesus. Jesus told her she has a wonderful heart and then Jesus was dancing with her. Grace was standing in the middle with Jesus dancing around her. She said it made her feel loved. Then she said that Jesus had written her name in a book and that book meant she was going to heaven.

Grace talked about all this the whole way home and still also when we were home and still when she was in bed. It was really significant for her. And then she prayed and thanked God for all this she experienced... It is so awesome!

I think it's awesome for her to experience God in this way, and I'm so grateful to our church, that it is an environment that kids (even in 'grown up' church) can feel His presence.

Grace has said to me that she has not felt God like that before.

God is doing good work in the kids of our church, and I truly believe you have been very instrumental in that... so thank you... Thank you that you have encouraged her, opened her to ideas and thoughts... I know without a doubt that what you do in kids church impacts the kids...

Story about Jessica age 8...

An extract from a stunningly beautiful conversation at bedtime tonight by a very peaceful, calm, contented daughter. She told this story a few times to me and also to Tim. Too busy abseiling last Sunday to tell us... and evidently a bit embarrassed.

'Last Sunday I became REAL friends with Jesus. I asked him into my heart like I hadn't before. All of this peace came. I felt like I was sitting on a chair on a balcony with beautiful doves flying all around me.

Then last night (Thursday) I was reading my bible about the man who fell asleep and stairs came near him and angels were going up and down. Then I fell asleep and stairs came outside my window (in our fairy garden) and angels came down. The big one, Gabriel, gave me a note. It said:

Dear.........., Thank you for becoming friends with Jesus.

And on the other side of the note it said: PS: Jesus and God are going to come and get you and show you up the stairs. I put the note into my pocket.

The angels went up the stairs and then Jesus and God came and got me. We went up the stairs and sat down under a tree and Jesus read me the Christmas story. Then they showed me a secret door into the cave and Gabriel showed me the actual bandages Jesus had. We went and had a look at the hill where the crosses were and Jesus showed me which one was his. Then we went on stairs and they showed me lots of rooms.

God showed me my own special room, just for me. It had my bed and Peter Rabbit and Mum and Dad. I saw Nan and Pop too. There was another massive room where people could just hang out with God.

Then he gave me another letter, saying 'thank you for coming to visit'. He gave me a special present. It is a key with my name on it, so I can come anytime I want.

I said 'thank you' and went back down the stairs with the angels. They tucked me into bed and read me the Easter story. They prayed for me and then I went to sleep.'

The interesting thing was that when Jess was telling me she said, 'Actually it felt like I was awake for the whole thing and when I got into bed I fell asleep, but actually I woke up then. It felt the opposite way – like I was awake for the dream part.'

This is from a girl who hadn't told us yet about her decision for Jesus, but has been up early and made her lunch and been dressed, etc. and done her brother's reader with him – almost every day this week. All before I was even up. A real change.

I am sure there is more coming. She is so excited about God and what is next.

Story about Ethan...

During the worship time, he felt that God told him that He was going to give him something. He opened his eyes and saw a little purple crystal in his palm. Shortly after, the purple crystal vanished bit by bit. Purple reminded him of 'royalty'; that Jesus is the King. The Lord spoke to him, saying that he is to put Jesus as first in his life because Jesus is King.

Jesus was the present arriving from the future. To live in the Spirit is to be aware of what is and what could be. God has made us a little lower than Himself (Psalm 8:5 NASB), yet the highest ambition for many believers is to be a little above the Joneses! Some Christians seem to have a greater desire to be 'good' than they have a desire for God (Psalm 42:1). When we desire God we quickly discover that promise and peril always co-exist. Jesus told Peter who he was and who he would be (Matthew 16:18). He spoke of the actual and the potential. In life it seems that the actual accuses and defies the potential. Often we only really find who we are in Christ as others nurture and believe in us. Jesus lived in a world of uncalculating generosity towards others. Examples are shown in the stories of the woman at the well, the woman caught in adultery, Zaccheus... and the list goes on. He was generous with the disciples as they learned what spirit they were of.

Discipleship that embraces a spirituality like Jesus' is daunting, because we have to develop senses that we are at best unfamiliar with and at worst we find difficult to believe in. The opportunity to be like Jesus in every way is fraught with the possibility of failure and embarrassment. For many of us, until recently, it was easier to retreat to the safety of a Christian life that avoided the unpredictability of the Spirit. We are turning this around as we pursue a life in community of being known, walking in humility and giving honour.

I asked our congregation – *What specific areas of your thinking have had to be renewed for you to step into believing heaven can invade earth through you?* Here are some of their responses:

Adoption and sonship...

I had not seen much of the power of God at work through me, outside of my own personal journey of healing. I felt I had all the faith in the world for healing, but when I prayed for people, only on a few occasions did healing occur. I eventually gave up, thinking that this was not a way God had chosen to use me.

The greatest breakthrough has come, I believe, in the revelation of partnership and sonship. This revelation has not come quickly. It has come in small steps that matched my own personal journey of inner healing. However, last year the Lord instructed me to spend the year in the book of Ephesians. As I did this the whole understanding of being a son, a child of adoption, just seemed to finally jell. The prayers in Ephesians1 and 3 became mine.

Partners through relationship...

One day as I was driving home I saw two eagles at close range. I was amazed and overwhelmed at their size. I knew it was a God encounter and that he wanted to show me something. He said 'K, I want you to learn two things from these eagles. First, the two are like you and me, we are partners through relationship. In everything you do, I am with you. Second, the eagle is absolutely confident in the way it has been designed. It doesn't doubt its ability to see from a long distance, or its ability to catch the wind and be led by the light of the sun. Be confident in the way I have designed you to partner with me as a much-loved son.'

That encounter really describes the transformation in my thinking, and now my behaviour. Confident to lean into Him, obey Him and enjoy the partnership through relationship.

God is responsible for the outcome, not me...

My responsibility in seeing heaven invade earth is to take every opportunity that comes across my path. To keep my eyes open to look for 'hurting' people, people in pain, people with broken bones, etc. and to keep the ears of my heart open for the Holy Spirit to nudge me. God's responsibility is for the outcome. I no longer have to be embarrassed that it may not work out, that the person may not get healed, that I might be embarrassed or harm God's reputation etc. God is always good. I need to leave the outcome to God. He knows the bigger picture. He is big enough to take care of His reputation if I am just doing what He has asked me to do in the Bible.

He needs us all...

The biggest change in my thinking has been around making mistakes on this journey. I remember being really worried about getting everything right, and this had the effect of stopping me moving into a place of being used by God to bring heaven to earth. If I can find the place where God loves me as a son and see how He has created me to be unique, then it becomes more obvious that He needs a multitude of different people to bring His expression on the earth. I have sometimes worried about being different and being on a different page to others. When I found the revelation that His Kingdom is a kaleidoscope of different expressions, and all of them are needed for the fullness of heaven to invade ALL the earth, [I knew] it means he needs all of us individually and collectively to create that expression.

Recognising lies and releasing truth...

In reflection, do I believe heaven can invade earth through me? That's the mindset that I struggled with, the 'through me' fear, I call it. Fear of the unknown, fear to present myself and face the fear of possible failure. The deceit of an un-truth, like, if I pray for them and they don't receive healing, how will they feel? No I won't pray for them just in case nothing happens; that way they won't get hurt. And you know, that's why I wouldn't let anyone pray for me. I didn't want to be disappointed; I felt that something was wrong with me and felt unworthy of receiving a blessing from God. I also felt that it was an embarrassment to them and me if nothing happened. It would cut deeply into one's belief, what a pack of deceitful lies I would tell myself. Fear is one of the biggest game breakers in a person's life.

With God's patient wisdom and understanding of my brokenness, I learnt to understand that 'through me' is an action, doing word an act of compassion, an act of obedience to God's great love, and that with gentle kindness He is leading me to express my heart's love and compassion as if we were one. He will only give you what you can handle.

If I have to think about moving to bring heaven down to earth then I will find a way not to do anything.

When God gives you a moment of compassion, that's your cue to get up and move, not to stop and justify. This is the area of thinking that I have had to renew.

My Dad loves me...

I've come to learn that through pursuing an intimate relationship with God and falling in love with Him, that He continues to challenge my thinking about myself and my identity. I was born into a very dysfunctional family so have had many 'broken' parts of my heart over the years to deal with, but learning to listen to the Lover of my soul constantly tell me how precious I am to Him and what He can do through me has shifted my mindset. It's like a paradigm shift – where you learn to think in a whole new way. In this case it was how I view myself and how I view Him. I'm able to shift the atmosphere because of Who I carry inside me, 'Greater is He that is in me than he who is in the world!'

Chapter Six

STYLE OF
COMMUNITY LIFE

As the crowning glory of creation, man was made in God's image, unencumbered by structure and free to simply 'be' in relationship with God and one another. When we truly learn to regard each other's concerns as significant as our own, the need for hierarchy diminishes.

– William P. Young –

The style of community life and resulting culture in a congregation is strongly influenced by the definition of what a disciple looks like. When a disciple of Jesus is defined as one who attends church regularly, tithes, participates in a small group, serves and practises spiritual disciplines, there will be a strong reliance on 'below the line' characteristics. As a result, community life and culture tends to be focused on hierarchy, the use of power and control to achieve conformity, and its functional relationships based on the performance of tasks and prioritising of programme development and growth in membership.

On the other hand, when a disciple of Jesus is defined as self-governing, innately powerful and inherently supernatural, there will be a strong reliance on 'above the line' characteristics. The resulting community life and culture will lean towards focusing on mutual accountability, collaboration, discussion based on shared values, heart relationships for the purpose of discovering identity and prioritising of hosting God's presence, and a naturally supernatural lifestyle.

Culture and community life are the consequence of what we believe, the values we as believers create and the behaviour that comes as we act on those beliefs. As a congregation grows in number, it is necessary to find ways of building the style of community and culture into the way new people are integrated and new initiatives and ministries are released. There are three areas that need to be attended to in order to ensure this happens. The first is to create common language for what is being pursued and what is being made. At Stairway this includes how we define a disciple: as someone who is self governing (exercising personal responsibility and self-awareness), innately powerful and inherently supernatural. Our common language is informed by 'above the line' characteristics. We maintain the regular use of the words identity, intimacy, inheritance and influence.

The second is the need to clearly define what the shared beliefs, values and behaviours are and have them in written form. You will find those of Stairway in Appendix One. These then become a natural part of the way we make decisions and build our yearly strategic plan and are the fundamentals that shape and form what is prioritised and what we pursue. They are our mandate, forming the basis for our mission and vision.

The third is the old maxim that you get what you measure. While measurement of 'below the line' characteristics remains important, an 'above the line' measurement commitment is our priority. Measurement 'below the line' is essentially easier because it is quantitative in nature. 'Above the line' measurement is far more qualitative. While describing a sunset can be subjective and open to interpretation, for most people the experience of the beauty is more meaningful than knowing the scientific facts that create the magnificent sky canvas preceding the onset of evening.

I asked our congregation this question: *Over the last five years how has your understanding of the normal Christian life changed and why?*

Here are some of their responses.

Talk without power is just talk...

Several years ago I was confronted by a renewed definition of what it meant to live a normal Christian life – when we began to emphasise this verse from 1 Corinthians 4:20, 'The Kingdom of God is not a matter of talk but of power'. It was confronting because I'm an articulate person who had been enjoying a lifestyle of sharing the gospel with others, regularly. The trouble was there was no power! As the emphasis grew, I refused to think about the chasm between my own experience and what the Bible was talking about. I was stuck.

About twelve months ago, I accidentally came across this verse again – deciding that I just couldn't ignore this any longer. I wanted to step from talk to power, but I was struggling to change this behaviour on my own. This involved putting myself on the line and leaving the outcome up to God and I was as nervous as a long-tailed cat in a room full of rocking chairs.

So I've begun asking some friends from our congregation to help me – friends who live the lifestyle I want to live. Several times now they've come with me to prophesy God's kindness over someone in the street or pray for healing for those with sickness. Now I can give a bunch of examples where my story reflected taking steps of risk and experiencing God's power touching someone... my lifestyle is beginning to align with the bible! I'm still growing in confidence to live a lifestyle of risk, but I do know that without the support and encouragement of my friends in this church, I would still be stuck back where I was.

Breath of life...

Over the last five years... I have realised that the supernatural breath of the Holy Spirit breathes life and this makes the difference to knowing and experiencing. It is great to have the head knowledge of what God can do and see it with your own eyes, but until the breath of the Holy Spirit breathes life and it sinks into your heart and becomes a living breathing experience it does not have the passion of God's heart that I am experiencing now. So in me there has been a change, individually, as God has provided a catalyst through the supernatural that melds together the creative and the spiritual, a new door has opened that I have never experienced before – painting prophetically, painting God's heart, painting a picture for a friend that would change their perspective on life and turn them around.

My 'Normal Christian Life' has been enriched and enlightened with knowing who I am as a child of God created in His image.

Journey to a Kingdom culture...

Throughout the last five years I have gained courage and experienced the power of God through personal healing, changed mindsets, and revelations of the Kingdom of God on earth. I am on a new journey in a new 'Kingdom Culture' that is bringing freedom from religion, establishing a core value system based on Jesus' thinking, not the church's or the world's thinking. I have radically been changed from the inside out. I continue to swim in an ocean of Joy and favour; I live under an umbrella of grace and view life with the eyes of mercy and in doing this I partner with Him to bring His will on earth as it is in Heaven.

Living my testimony...

In the last 2-3 years my understanding of a normal Christian life has dramatically changed. I had spent some fifty years in a conservative denominational church. I was not well informed on matters of the Holy Spirit and the associated gifts. I now realise that the things that Jesus did every day are how we should be operating and am praying for work colleagues for healings. In home group we prayed for one of the group and the swelling in his neck had decreased significantly before the end of the night and his fever had gone.

I have also had words for people that I was not sure about, but subsequently they have been confirmed so I am getting excited about the future and what God might want me to do. I took part in the healing nights last year and saw some amazing things happen in getting words for people and healings. During the Supernatural Healing course I was actually healed of my severe food allergies. This has not been an issue for me now for the last six months. I am starting to pray for others with allergy problems so they can live in my testimony.

Trusting God and not a diagnosis...

God has transformed my thinking hugely over the last three and a half years, particularly in the area of healing. When faced with having my unborn baby come into the world with possible brain abnormalities and other genetic problems I had to make a decision. Do I believe the bible and all that God says and go after healing or do I take on a medical view and diagnosis?

I learned to fill my heart and mind each day with scripture, song and a crafted prayer that declared healing that were in line with what God says and not meditate on the problems/diagnosis.

I have learned that we don't need to ask or beg God for healing; healing has already happened at the cross... 'by Jesus' stripes we are healed'. I started to thank God it had already been done, gave praise everyday for what I was believing for and made sure that my thinking was in line with the healing that had already taken place! I then prayed for positive medical reports. Six weeks later we got our first positive medical report. A few weeks later my healthy baby boy was born! We had to have a follow up scan six weeks postnatally and so we then went after more positive medical reports. We had the scan and our beautiful boy was given yet another positive medical report!

The biggest change in me would be my disposition when faced with difficult situations and live circumstances. Not trying to fix everything myself and relying on my own ability to get things done, but to trust in God and ALWAYS choose PEACE and JOY no matter what. Keeping a thankful, worshipful heart and knowing God has everything under control!

At this point it will be helpful to again revisit some of my previous thoughts from *Above the Line*. This matter of style of community and culture has continued to emerge as being significant in how we make a disciple.

Jesus' declaration that everything in the Kingdom of God would be fulfilled through pursuing the two great commandments squarely places the emphasis on relationships. Relationship with God, relationships with others and relationship with self should be our priority. We should prioritise developing the skills, attitudes and awareness that will release us into relationships of unconditional love.

I wonder what would happen if God's people rigorously pursued the ideals of 1 Corinthians 13:4–8 and Colossians 3:12–17, below. I wonder about the live and vibrancy of local churches, if people dared to believe that they could shape their self-talk and self-awareness to these ideals.

Love is patient, love is kind and is not jealous; love does not brag and is not arrogant, does not act unbecomingly; it does not seek its own, is not provoked, does not take into account a wrong suffered, does not rejoice in unrighteousness, but rejoices with the truth; bears all things, believes all things, hopes all things, endures all things. Love never fails; but if there are gifts of prophecy, they will be done away; if there are tongues, they will cease; if there is knowledge, it will be done away. (1 Corinthians 13:4-8)

So, as those who have been chosen of God, holy and beloved, put on a heart of compassion, kindness, humility, gentleness and patience;

bearing with one another, and forgiving each other, whoever has a complaint against anyone; just as the Lord forgave you, so also should you. Beyond all these things put on love, which is the perfect bond of unity. Let the peace of Christ rule in your hearts, to which indeed you were called in one body; and be thankful. Let the word of Christ richly dwell within you, with all wisdom teaching and admonishing one another with psalms and hymns and spiritual songs, singing with thankfulness in your hearts to God. Whatever you do in word or deed, do all in the name of the Lord Jesus, giving thanks through Him to God the Father. (Colossians 3:12-17)

What if these two sets of scripture were the grid through which we assessed our attitudes and behaviour towards every person we met and lived with? What if they were the reference point we used in deciding how we would respond to others when there was tension, conflict, disagreement and failure? In other words, what if we were *always* motivated to prioritise and protect relationships before trying to be right or get our way without consideration of the impact that has on others. We protect our relationships by learning how to live with another's 'ideas'. That is, how do they perceive the circumstances that are being experienced by us and communication that is taking place? We focus on their interests, not just our own, in finding the common ground to move into the future with love, honour and respect for all concerned.

There is considerable evidence within church life, Christian living and Kingdom activity that prioritising and protecting relationships regularly falls off the agenda. There are the pastors who go away on leave only to return to find they are no longer considered suitable for their role. There are pastors who use their authority and power to get their own way. There are members of the congregation who oppose the pastor, citing isolated events or giving minimal proof to support their criticism. Inflammatory emails are exchanged between church leaders, disgruntled at the way some aspects of the ministry are being managed. Male pastors leave their wives for a female member of staff. Pastors' children rebel due to a lack of relationship with their dads, whose zeal and committed attention to the work of the ministry results in a love deficit to their family members. The list is seemingly endless.

Interestingly, the range of excuses for behaving in these ways is also seemingly endless. The art of justification has been mastered all-too-well by many of us. It gives us permission to act outside the way of God's Kingdom. Judging and criticising others are stand out examples. But scripture is clear:

> 'Do not judge so that you will not be judged. 2 'For in the way you judge, you will be judged; and by your standard of measure, it will be measured to you. 3 'Why do you look at the speck that is in your brother's eye, but do not notice the log that is in your own eye? 'Or how can you say to your brother, 'Let me take the speck out of your eye,' and behold, the log is in your own eye? 'You hypocrite, first take the log out of your own eye, and then you will see clearly to take the speck out of your brother's eye.' (Matthew 7:1-5)

Yet lovers of God will find ways of excusing this sort of behaviour, from the lame to the sophisticated. Rather than develop self-awareness about what is influencing their perception, they take the easy way out by ascribing intent and motive to others. Instead of taking personal responsibility for their own lack of obedience to scripture, they rely on the 'should' and 'could' family of words. We all have a justice meter finely tuned in different situations to the way others are not meeting our expectations. When this is switched on, we can be quick to respond with a 'tell and demand' style of communication. That is, 'let me tell you what you have done that is inappropriate and then I will demand that you do or say something to remedy the damage I think you have caused.' The net result is a prioritising of justice over understanding, recognising that things can be understandable and yet not acceptable. In contrast the pursuit of understanding will protect a relationship. Understanding is pursued by a communication style which relies upon observation and questions. That is, 'I observe this has happened, can you help me understand why?'

There is great complexity in the uniqueness of what motivates each individual's response and reactions. It is only through developing self-awareness, often initiated by the Holy Spirit, and then taking personal responsibility for our own contribution to the damage caused in a relationship, that we learn how to practise the fruit of the Spirit (Galatians 5: 22–24). However, in our congregation we are discovering in our focus on the above the line attributes that there are two general themes which help in prioritising and protecting relationships. The first is understanding the biblical pattern of two governments in the way the Lord approaches the regulation of our behaviour. The second is revisiting the way we define the word honour and its implications for the development of strong relationships.

When it comes to the regulation of our behaviour the Old Testament has a focus on the law and the New Testament has a focus on grace. Paul, in the book of Galatians, articulates this shift.

He identifies that in the Old Testament God relied on an external governing system of rules. He demanded obedience and conformity as the way of regulating the behaviour of His people. Consequently, it could be said that He had a government of rules. Paul contrasts this with the New Testament where God now relies on an internal governing system of love and grace. He now relies on us to draw from the love and freedom we have received from Him to regulate our behaviour. Now love is the motivation to prioritise and protect relationships. Consequently, it could be said that He now has a government of love. (Isaiah 16:5).

Paul writes:

But before faith came, we were kept in custody under the law, being shut up to the faith which was later to be revealed. Therefore the Law has become our tutor to lead us to Christ, so that we may be justified by faith. But now that faith has come, we are no longer under a tutor. For you are all sons of God through faith in Christ Jesus. (Galatians 3:23-26)

So, in the Old Testament the motivating force for God's people to regulate their behaviour came in the form of blessing for obedience and threats of punishment for disobedience. In the New Testament the motivating force in the life of a believer to regulate their behaviour comes from a passion for God after encountering His love. God is dwelling in us, creating places where we know His love and we can now respond from there. In Jeremiah 31:27–34 the prophet saw into the future and recognised this change was in the heart of God. These thoughts are summarised in the following diagram.

OLD TESTAMENT	NEW TESTAMENT
▼	▼
Focus on: Conformity / Rules / Obedience	Focus on: Loving each other / Protecting relationships that bring freedom
▼	▼
Government of rules	Government of love
▼	▼
External governing system	Internal governing system

Jeremiah 31: 27 – 34

▼	▼
Some consequences	Some consequences
1. Agree with rules – everything OK Disagree with rules – punished	1. Understanding each other's need to look out for individual interest
2. One party more powerful	2. Everyone equally powerful
3. Control others through rules	3. Manage self to protect relationships
▼	▼
Predisposition to Control	Predisposition to Honour

DIAGRAM 4

To move towards primarily living above the line, it is necessary to pursue love and relationships above obedience and compliance. However, many of us were raised by parents whose goal was obedience and compliance on our part. That is, we were shown what was good and bad and coerced or 'managed' in some way to choose good. Consequently rules were elevated above relationship.

Personal responsibility was undermined through the experience that someone else was responsible to make us do what was right. Our obedience was based more on duty and expectation than passion and a desire to protect the heart of our parents. Authority figures (including God) are traditionally seen as enforcers of punishment to be feared, rather than understanding, caring and concerned individuals.

These beliefs now, at times subconsciously, inform our behaviour, inevitably drawing us into a culture that is dominated by a government of rules. With this reality it is safer to stay focussed below the line as less personal and organisational transformation is required. We tolerate an understanding of relationships and community where:

- We are all protecting ourselves, struggling to find value, enduring superficial connection and wondering why it is difficult to find unity.
- Motives and character are judged so as to invalidate another's perspective.
- When we feel powerless we reach out for what makes us powerful, which is normally a willingness to hurt others or at least an implied threat to hurt others.
- If we feel scared, anxious or fearful we will default to a range of methods to feel in control and even punish others.
- There is a lack of personal responsibility on the basis that someone else didn't control us by doing something for us, so they are responsible.

- The ultimate form of control is a call for 'honour' that is defined as someone with less power surrendering to someone with more power.

With the above in mind love is expressed and experienced to varying degrees in the context of rules. The church, on the basis of pursuing holiness, righteousness and correct order has many rules. The church will both consciously and unconsciously use the experience of the Old Testament to judge rule-breakers. We are better at punishing those who disagree with us than taking the time to understand their point of view. For some, loyalty is defined as agreement, therefore disagreement is viewed as disloyalty, often deserving of correction. The church is famous for shooting its wounded. It is often more judgemental than those outside its domain and influence.

In creating a culture that supports the two great commandments we, like James and John (Luke 9: 51–56) are confronted with the need to change our way of thinking. We need to think and act out of the Spirit of Jesus. We are not intended to destroy, but to serve through love. We so easily establish a government of rules because that is what we are familiar with. Yet in doing so we often become pharisaical and bound by law and religion in the way we approach relationships.

There is a new covenant based in love that is to motivate how we define relationships and community. It is not a 'new' old covenant that hangs onto rules, conformity and judgement. The new covenant requires a different mindset, different goals and a new skill set. The old skills of control, power and punishment developed in our upbringing under a government of rules must change. Jesus died for our freedom, not our control. The new skill set of taking into account the interests of others, mutual submission and true forgiveness can be better learned when biblical honour is understood.

Love expects that we will pursue an extraordinary awareness of others so that we can be led by the Spirit to places of self sacrifice. The style of community that creates a culture where the normal Christian life is to be like Jesus in every way is built on a commitment to awareness of others so that the Spirit can bring freedom to all.

Freedom is grounded in the knowledge of how much we have been forgiven. A reality that exists at the core of our being that God accepts me and delights in me as I am. We begin to trust the warmth and spontaneity of God's love for us. We live with an awareness that forgiveness is a continuous and ceaseless flow of loving acceptance that empowers us to break free of our sin, changing our behaviour and attitudes so that we can be like Jesus in every way. From this place we are prepared to live with a love for the Lord and a love for people that can demand everything we have.

Freedom is grounded in the truth. We can discover the truth of the Word for ourselves as we concentrate on it, listen to it and look at the reflection in which we do or don't see ourselves. The bible is the record of Jesus' love affair with each human being and the record has been personally applied and accepted. We can't be free when we have to refer to some other source of authority or seek some one else's approval. Jesus is the way, the truth and the life and it is because of this that He is the only one who brings true and lasting freedom.

A few years ago we had the opportunity to visit the Uffizi art gallery in Florence. The quantity and quality of the art was extraordinary. It would have been necessary to spend an entire week, eight hours a day to even begin to appreciate all that was on display. I was fascinated by the two types of people in the gallery. There were those who predominantly walked around with their heads buried in a guide book reading about the artworks, while occasionally looking up at them; others simply walked and looked, allowing the artworks to speak for themselves. The opinion of others is helpful but the heart-felt experience and encounter is saved for those who engage personally.

Freedom is grounded in direct access to God. The Holy Spirit brings Jesus ceaselessly to our remembrance to live and make choices with reference to Him. A spirituality which requires an institution or group to determine what is good and evil implies that we can know ourselves outside of our relationship with God. Self-reference through the expectations or requirements of others only leads to the law and a life of works. The freedom offered by following Jesus is discovered by learning how to abide in Jesus rather than be dictated to by the belief system of others.

As we build communities of faith which long for everyone to find their freedom in the Spirit through forgiveness, being grounded in the truth and living with the expectation of direct access to God, we facilitate the opportunity for the normal Christian life to be living like Jesus in every way.

Another aspect of the style of community life in a congregation that releases people to be like Jesus in every way, is to highly value that truth that we are to be the Holy Spirit's inexhaustible fuel for his mission in the world. There must be a culture that expresses the idea that the Spirit has been given to the church and therefore the church (the people and their organising principles) must be given to the Spirit.

To achieve this end, it is imperative that the words and actions of all in the community reinforce the truth that the Spirit leads us to *be*, and then to *do*. We must allow ourselves, and also allow others, to live the kingdom life as free sons of God. We must collectively pursue the truth about Jesus. The context for all acts of service, whether within or outside the congregation, is Jesus' victory over the devil. We must help one another to be sensitive to the reality of others before trying to solve problems, while all the time discerning what God is doing in every situation on the basis of freedom, awareness and self-sacrifice. Once our discernment has discovered what God is doing, we join ourselves to that.

Discernment is facilitated by the knowledge that God *allows* in His wisdom that which could be prevented by His power. We should examine our circumstances to discover what is being done *to* us so we can learn to respond like Jesus. If we instead focus on what *we* can do *about* our circumstances, we are prone to seeking an answer of the flesh. What we know about Jesus empowers us, and therefore our response to discerning what is taking place in our circumstances and relationship needs to include investigating these questions:

- Who does Jesus want to be for me in this that He couldn't otherwise be?
- What must I do?; and,
- What does this mean?

As we make these issues one of the foundations for the style of community in which to make disciples, then we will more readily become that inexhaustible fuel for the Spirit's mission in the world.

Here are some stories of what God is doing through His people.

A cuppa with no lumps...

I heard today that a woman I prayed for some months ago in the Newcomers Lounge was healed. She had a lump in her throat and after prayer went to the GP and it had gone. She is now attending Stairway regularly.

Wheelchair permanently parked...

Just thought you would like to read this below – we got another one!

This is the first lady I prayed for a few years back while on tour in Qld. I told her God would heal her and we prayed for her and then I walked with her.

Well she got it! God is good.

Hi R,

How are you? GUESS WHAT? Your prophecy came true – wheelchair is in our garage!!!! God has healed me! Praise Him!

Baby dream a reality...

My cousin J and his wife S had been trying for three years to conceive a baby with no luck. They had all sorts of tests done only to be told they couldn't see a problem, but the likelihood of them conceiving was slim to none. They started fertility treatments but that didn't work either. They were very disappointed and thought they would never have the baby they dreamed of. I asked them if they'd come to my house and let me, C and R (also from Stairway) gather together in prayer to believe for a baby and lay hands on them.

After our prayer night S conceived naturally in her very next cycle. She had a healthy pregnancy as we had prayed and a very straightforward natural labour as we had also believed God for. Their baby girl A, was born a few weeks earlier than her due date. She came exactly nine months to the day after the prayer night we had! God is amazing!

Student becomes teacher...

My Christian Ed. teacher had something wrong with the discs in his back and said that he was going to have surgery soon.

I had a feeling that God wanted me to pray for him. I didn't really want to, so I just kind of left it. The next day I felt really nervous and sick (that's how I feel God) so I went up to him and said that God wanted me to pray for him and he said cool, so I prayed for him, also praying that he didn't have to have the surgery.

Afterwards I didn't know how it ended up but I didn't really care because I knew God wanted me to pray for him and even though he is my Christian Studies teacher, it still counted for me that I was brave enough to do it.

He came up to me before class yesterday and said 'E, can I speak to you for a minute.' I thought 'Oh crap, I'm in trouble', and he said that my prayer worked and that he doesn't have to have surgery now! He had gone to the surgeon's to have a final check and plan for the surgery and have more x-rays. The x-rays were completely clear and he knew straight away that it was the prayer that made the difference.

He seemed really happy, so I am really glad that I did it.

The final thing I want to highlight that influences the style of community life in a congregation that releases people to be like Jesus in every way, is to live towards each other without rules. Instead, we discover a set of values that release freedom and truth. Such an approach requires us to trust the Holy Spirit to both lead us to these values and develop them in us. We can then build community by having a style of life in our hearts, not rules for life. Such a stance fosters the more spontaneous obedience that marks a spirit filled life.

The values I speak of here are the values of the person you should aim to be when under stress. They empower us when tension exists in a relationship because we have decided to prosper, rather than succumb, to tension. We are looking to see how we can be like Jesus when we are under pressure. We have a prepared commitment to bring conflict and tension under the influence of these values.

These values prompt us to seek the source of our responses rather than reacting to the external circumstances that are initiating the response. Such a response acknowledges that tension does not mean something is wrong. Rather, it means that something is happening. It also brings a focus on discovery, rather than defence, in relationships.

We have every opportunity to bring this focus on discovery to our responses when we are offended. When there is potential to take offence, my values are:

- Taking offence can be understandable but it can never be acceptable.
- Being offended is always valid in the eyes of the person offended.
- When I agree with another's offensive stance, I imprison them further.
- One of the tests for receiving more of the kingdom is to handle the taking of offence properly.
- Taking offence can become an excuse to not become who God is calling me to be, and as a consequence His dream will be hindered.

When I hold to these values, I now know how not to respond in this place of pressure! Opportunities to be offended are always going to come and we need to have a positive set of values to counteract offence at those times.

Philippians 4:8 reminds us to focus on the good person behind the bad behaviour:

Finally, brethren, whatever is true, whatever is honourable, whatever is right, whatever is pure, whatever is lovely, whatever is of good repute, if there is any excellence and if anything worthy of praise, dwell on these things.

When I honour people who have initiated offence I elevate their status from judged to forgiven; I glory in who they are and promote their well-being by seeing the positive of who they are and highlighting them; I give them prestige by recognising they are loved and cherished by God and so will be by me; and, I respect and admire them by protecting them from my pain.

1 Corinthians 13:4–8 clarifies this point further:

Love is patient, love is kind and is not jealous; love does not brag and is not arrogant, does not act unbecomingly; it does not seek its own, is not provoked, does not take into account a wrong suffered, does not rejoice in unrighteousness, but rejoices with the truth; bears all things, believes all things, hopes all things, endures all things.

Love never fails; but if there are gifts of prophecy, they will be done away; if there are tongues, they will cease; if there is knowledge, it will be done away.

1 Peter 5:5–7 asks us to practise humility:

You younger men, likewise, be subject to your elders; and all of you, clothe yourselves with humility toward one another, for God is opposed to the proud, but gives grace to the humble.

Therefore humble yourselves under the mighty hand of God, that He may exalt you at the proper time, casting all your anxiety on Him, because He cares for you.

I choose to go lower still in avoiding the *need to be right* because doing so summons the responses from my justice meter, that is, the internal yardstick we use to decide if others are right or wrong, good or bad, valuable or disposable. It's that inner scale that determines our level of judgment and criticism of others as we assess the appropriateness of their actions or behaviour.

These values are created because we observe that Jesus was never a victim of His circumstances: rather, He is always freely responsible. Jesus' way of obedience was to follow the Spirit, not some external moral code. Jesus' response was always to do the most loving thing, as illustrated by John 8:3–11.

The scribes and the Pharisees *brought a woman caught in adultery, and having set her in the center of the court, they *said to Him, "Teacher, this woman has been caught in adultery, in the very act. Now in the Law Moses commanded us to stone such women; what then do You say?" They were saying this, testing Him, so that they might have grounds for accusing Him. But Jesus stooped down and with His finger wrote on the ground. But when they persisted in asking Him, He straightened up, and said to them, "He who is without sin among you, let him be the first to throw a stone at her." *Again He stooped down and wrote on the ground. When they heard it, they began to go out one by one, beginning with the older ones, and He was left alone, and the woman, where she was, in the center of the court. Straightening up, Jesus said to her, "Woman, where are they? Did no one condemn you?" She said, "No one, Lord." And Jesus said, "I do not condemn you, either. Go. From now on sin no more."*

Chapter Seven
PROPHETIC
EMPOWERMENT

You can't solve a problem with the same mindset that created it

– Einstein –

The purpose of God is to bring many sons into glory; to release us into being increasingly in His image; and, to be overcomers learning to become more than conquerors. God is intentional in His purpose and so must we be.

The Genesis story reveals that God created man for fellowship with Him and to rule the earth on God's behalf. Adam and Eve's sin caused this dream to be temporarily impeded. Yet God is relentless in His devotion to see His dream fulfilled and release mankind to live and reign with Him.

For if by the transgression of the one, death reigned through the one, much more those who receive the abundance of grace and of the gift of righteousness will reign in life through the One, Jesus Christ.

So then as through one transgression there resulted condemnation to all men, even so through one act of righteousness there resulted justification of life to all men. For as through the one man's disobedience the many were made sinners, even so through the obedience of the One the many will be made righteous. (Romans 5:17–19)

As Adam represented humanity, so Jesus as the new Adam represents humanity. With God, life engulfs death. The new representative overwhelms the old representative. The new creation identity is to replace the first creation identity.

Therefore if anyone is in Christ, he is a new creature; the old things passed away; behold, new things have come. (2 Corinthians 5:17)

THE NEW CREATION MIRACLE

The new creation miracle changes everything for those who are born again. We are now *created in Christ* (Ephesians 2:10); we are *created in righteousness* (Ephesians 4:24) and we are definitely *new creations* (Galatians 6:15). The result is that Christ is in us (Colossians 1:27) and we have the mind of Christ (1 Corinthians 2:16). When we allow the miracle of new creation to penetrate the depths of our being it changes everything about how we embrace and conduct our lives. The flow on of the new creation miracle is that we have received every spiritual blessing (Ephesians 1:3), and we have been granted everything that pertains to life and godliness (2 Peter 1:3). Thus a beachhead of heaven has been established in us (Romans 8:10, Galatians 3:26) releasing us to be spiritual beings enjoying supernatural experiences as we discover how heaven can invade earth through us.

As followers of Jesus we can be confused about our true identity because while the work in our spirit is finished (Colossians 2:11–14), the work in our soul is in progress (Ephesians 4:22–24). Colossians 2:11–14, in the New Living Translation declares:

When you came to Christ, you were "circumcised," but not by a physical procedure. Christ performed a spiritual circumcision— the cutting away of your sinful nature. For you were buried with Christ when you were baptized. And with him you were raised to new life because you trusted the mighty power of God, who raised Christ from the dead.

You were dead because of your sins and because your sinful nature was not yet cut away. Then God made you alive with Christ, for he forgave all our sins. He cancelled the record of the charges against us and took it away by nailing it to the cross.

The cutting away of the sin nature is not a metaphor; it is a reality. We are a new creation in our spirit, yet Ephesians 4:22–24 clearly illustrates that our soul, (our mind, will and emotions), is catching up to the new creation reality:

that, in reference to your former manner of life, you lay aside the old self, which is being corrupted in accordance with the lusts of deceit, and that you be renewed in the spirit of your mind, and put on the new self, which in the likeness of God has been created in righteousness and holiness of the truth.

This helps to explain why Paul declares that on the one hand 'we are something' and on the other hand 'we are becoming the same thing'! Let me illustrate:

1. We are sanctified in Christ (1 Corinthians 1:2 and 6:11); and we are being sanctified (Hebrews 2:11 and 10:14)

2. We are holy in Christ (Colossians 1:22; Hebrews 3:1); and we are called to be holy (1 Thessalonians 3:13 ; 2 Corinthians 7:1)

3. We are the righteousness of Christ (2 Corinthians 5:21); and we are called to pursue righteousness (2 Timothy 2:22).

Stated simply, our spirit has a new creation identity while our soul is still undergoing supernatural transformation into its identity. This is why Paul writes:

And do not be conformed to this world, but be transformed by the renewing of your mind, so that you may prove what the will of God is, that which is good and acceptable and perfect. (Romans 12:2)

But we all, with unveiled face, beholding as in a mirror the glory of the Lord, are being transformed into the same image from glory to glory, just as from the Lord, the Spirit. (2 Corinthians 3:18)

So we are learning to live in the reality of our new identity and walk in it. We are discovering how to deflect false identities in our self-talk and un-renewed mind. We are in process with God so that our soul catches up to the miracle in our spirit.

God wants to colonise the earth with people who represent heaven. The devil doesn't want us to learn to live in the reality of our new identity because then we will walk in the same manner Jesus walked (1 John 2:6) and do the works that Jesus did and even greater (John 14:12). (See the story below and more in Chapter Eight.)

Bringing the presence of God in a desolate place...

I recently just started a new job at a mental hospital in the city.

I am working in the adult unit, the most acute floor, which comprises patients from the ages of 19–40, all with severe mental illness that incapacitates their lives.

The majority of these patients are women, who have experienced devastating trauma, abuse and neglect. Some stories have actually been too painful to listen to...

The scope of practice in this facility is favourably wide and I have found myself being able to speak God's words of life over people every day. Each day there is a breakthrough, each day I am able to bring in His presence. Each day I am amazed at how He moves... too many stories to mention.

Something needs to be done... the army needs to be bigger, wider, stronger...

I find it an incredible privilege to part of this ministry and know that I have been equipped by being part of Stairway. I walk in the authority that I have received not only from Him but from the revelatory teaching and tangible presence that I have encountered in our church.

INTENTIONALLY ENGAGE WITH YOUR PROPHETIC WORDS

The process is fuelled and inspired by the word of God. Deuteronomy 8:3 says:

He humbled you and let you be hungry, and fed you with manna which you did not know, nor did your fathers know, that He might make you understand that man does not live by bread alone, but man lives by everything that proceeds out of the mouth of the LORD.

So, we are to align our thoughts and words about who we are and who God is for us with what the bible says. We are to agree with God allowing the spirit of wisdom and revelation to release grace so that our heart beliefs and attitudes change. This principle applies to both the 'eternal' word of God in the bible and the 'now' words of God we receive through prophetic utterances.

1 Timothy 1:18 is helpful here:

This command I entrust to you, Timothy, my son, in accordance with the prophecies previously made concerning you, that by them you fight the good fight,

The journey of disciple making that releases a normal Christian life of heaven invading earth through us is enhanced, empowered and equipped by closing the gap between prophecy spoken and prophecy fulfilled. Prophetic words demand discovery and require process. So much of God's activity in our lives is connected to Him intentionally establishing within us the identity He has called us to (2 Samuel 9:1–8). We are led by the Spirit to accept His vision of us and how He sees us. We are learning to agree with His preferred identity for us. What God sees over us we are to see. Exodus 7:1 teaches us that we need to see a thing in order to become it.

> *Then the Lord said to Moses, 'See, I make you as God to Pharaoh, and your brother Aaron shall be your prophet'.*

That is, unless Moses saw himself as God saw him, he would not have the courage to stand before Pharaoh.

Prophetic words are markers for what is possible (Jeremiah 29:11). Prophetic words create a horizon to bring back to the present. Prophetic words declare what God thinks about us and our circumstances. They point to territory to be pursued and taken. Prophetic words link your significant present with God's preferred future.

God wants to interact with us as the person of the future. He is calling us up into how He sees us and releasing us into a significant life of co-labouring with Him. Consequently we need to be attentive to the ways God engages with us so that we undertake the journey well. At Stairway we have discovered that we need to:

- live in the moment with God and make choices to participate;
- understand the lesson we are in and co-operate with the Spirit;
- try to see what God is doing and learning what we need;
- determining to discern and choose the intention of God towards us in the moment; and,
- understand the mind of the Lord, discovering how He thinks and the way He likes to do things.

Graham Cooke says it this way:

> Focus on the experience of His nature towards you. What is it that he wants to be for you now? He will always reveal His intention. He is continuously fixed on His outcome for you. He is choosing to make you like Him. Therefore, He allows in His wisdom what He could easily prevent by His power. He chooses our situations to empower us to rise up in his intentional identity in us and intention is our identity. Our choosing, then, is much more powerful than we can imagine.

ENGAGING WITH THE PROCESS

To facilitate the discovery and process of seeing our prophetic words fulfilled we need to embrace:

- a series of steps required to get there;
- the imperative and necessity of learning curves;
- the place of exploring the dimensions of self that God is calling us to;
- the importance of who we are becoming and what kind of person we need to become in order for the prophecy to be fulfilled;
- what is required to grow in favour, authority and intimacy; and,
- bringing into the present the qualities and characteristics of the person God sees in the future and practising them now.

There are a range of practical things to undertake and mind-sets to bring into the process, especially:

- writing out the prophetic words you have been given either with paragraph headings or using bullet points;
- looking for what is repeated in a word or over a number of words:
  - Key words;
  - Key phrases;
  - Character needed.

The process will make us richer. It provides the vehicle to see ourselves as He sees us and to move towards what God has promised. To that end, I urge you to see the process as an ongoing encounter not an event. Take responsibility for your prophetic words. Go after places of stubborn resistance. We are not part of an audience we are part of an army. Learn obedience. Be responsive to the Lord. Embrace vulnerability to the goodness of God as a way of life. Deal with passivity and procrastination and celebrate His intentions. Align yourself to the spirit of promise, the nature of God and the process of being upgraded in your partnership with Him!

ELEMENTS OF THE PROCESS

Intimacy and Abiding

God is not available to the casual seeker (Jeremiah 29:13). We discover prophetic intent through being established in intimacy with God and pursuing fellowship with God. We are to practise trusting God, being faithful to Him, stirring up our affection towards Him, exploring the deep affection of God and expressing adoration of Him because He adores us. Prophecy should create a hunger for intimacy and fulfilment.

Abiding is the key to becoming. Therefore there is a need to interact with prophecy in the inner man to keep it alive, fresh and dynamic. Intimacy positions us to embrace the fullness of God's favour resulting in God sponsoring us. Every interaction is concerned with abiding. Learning to stay in rest and participate from a place of agreement and alignment. Are your current choices in life coming from an understanding of your lot in this world or are they arising out of a place of agreement regarding your place in the Kingdom?

Testing

Tests develop us to become who we need to be in the future. Circumstances are to be the making of you, not the death of you. Giants are to be defeated. Tests are an opportunity for God to show who He is for us and for us to see who we are becoming in Him. Testing is concerned with receiving; it is the territory where we learn to put off the old and put on the new.

Prophetic words play a critical part in the way we respond to testing.

1 Timothy 1:18 calls us to go to war with our prophecies. Prophecy helps us to know how to respond to the test and co-operate with God. Prophecy helps us to stand, walk and press in during tests. It brings focus to tests of character, lifestyle and belief. Prophecy helps us to live in the truth of God's word as it is unfolding. Joseph's life is a great testament to this.

Prophecy provides favour in tests. Prophecy speaks of an all-knowing God of whom I am in awe, which in turn helps me to defeat circumstances *because* I know He is big! Prophecy helps to guide my perspective, where I look from and what I look at when tested. Tests handled this way consummate prophecy in our hearts that then births the lifestyle of who we need to be. We see this most visibly in David's life.

Weaknesses

We are often called to do what is utterly impossible without God. Such calls highlight the reasons why we can't be and do what God is asking. It shines light onto what we are not. Prophecy tells us we will survive the process of addressing our weaknesses and shortcomings. Prophecy helps us to stare down limitations and inadequacies by adopting a joyful vulnerability. Prophecy releases an attitude of being at ease with our lowest state of being so that He can be who He wants to be for us.

Our life with God is an unfolding of our identity and inheritance. We are to learn by process the nature, promises and victory of God. When things go wrong, He wants us to stand on our prophetic words, fight and contend for His preferred future and to discover what He is teaching us in warfare. Prophetic words help us to use the lens of God's perspective through which to view our current circumstances and avoid seeking answers in our own strength.

At this point, I would like to express a huge thank you to my good friend Graham Cooke for all he has brought to us. His insights and wisdom are strongly reflected in this chapter.

Chapter Eight

TESTIMONIAL
ENCOURAGEMENT

We will not conceal them from their children,

But tell to the generation to come the praises of the LORD,

And His strength and His wondrous works that He has done.

For He established a testimony in Jacob

And appointed a law in Israel,

Which He commanded our fathers

That they should teach them to their children,

That the generation to come might know, even the children yet to be born,

That they may arise and tell them to their children,

That they should put their confidence in God

And not forget the works of God,

But keep His commandments,

And not be like their fathers,

A stubborn and rebellious generation,

A generation that did not prepare its heart

And whose spirit was not faithful to God.

The sons of Ephraim were archers equipped with bows,

Yet they turned back in the day of battle.

They did not keep the covenant of God

And refused to walk in His law;

They forgot His deeds

And His miracles that He had shown them.

– Psalm 78: 4-11 –

We have discovered the power of testimony to do many things, that give glory to God. These deeds inspire faith. They generate the thought that 'if that can happen for them, it can happen for me'. They are prophetic and open up realms of the impossible to be duplicated. They stir our affection for God; who He is and who we are in Him. They demonstrate what we hold up as the normal Christian life. They speak of possibility. They declare: 'this is who we are', and encourage us to 'become'. They stop us falling back into programmes, structure and our own effort as the primary way of making a life together.

As a faith community we are making disciples of the Kingdom of God. We are emphasising what Jesus emphasised. We want to look at Jesus to discover how to be like Him. When we focus on what He has done and is doing, we are looking at Him. As we look upon Him it ignites inspiration to be like Him.

While I have provided stories and examples of what we have learned throughout this book, I believe a whole chapter of them will be inspiring and lift you into great places and possibilities with God. When we first began the journey that resulted in the writing of this book, we did not have many of our own stories, so we told the stories of other churches. Telling those external stories encouraged and inspired us enormously to continue our journey and begin amassing our own. So now, I trust our stories will encourage you to continue or begin your own journey.

A SELECTION FROM THE MANY TESTIMONIES AT STAIRWAY

God brings them to my door...

Ahmed and Chris came to fix some curtains that had been playing up for months – it had been a most frustrating process, but through this time God surely had something brewing, because, if there been no problem with the curtain rod, Ahmed would not have been at my house for me to pray for him.

The team were replacing the rod when Ahmed said he was not doing any physical work because he had torn all the ligaments in his shoulder – it was sore and he could not lift it or move it at all.

I asked him if I could pray for him. He agreed and I started to pray with my hand on his shoulder – feeling apprehensive and hoping God would show up. I felt nothing and was nervous... this was a complete stranger... but as I continued (rebuking the battle in my head) I gradually began to feel warmth under my hand and asked him if he could too. He said 'yes' and so, feeling encouraged, I kept praying and then asked him to check it out. He said it was much better and he had better movement. He said the pain and lack of movement was a 7; whereas, before, it was a 10.

I said, 'let's keep praying' and as I prayed again I felt the warmth again. I prayed quietly that he would have dreams and visions and see the truth about God and kept praying for and releasing healing, releasing the Holy Spirit on and in him. The warmth continued.

He then tried it out again and said 'gosh' and tentatively moved it above his head in circular movements... with a look of surprise – he had not been able to raise his arm without pain before I had prayed.

I prayed again to rid him of the remnant of the pain and I then left him to it – raising his arm above his head, looking amazed.

185

Department store destiny...

I headed up to the Myer car park, feeling that I was to walk through Myer's on the way to the shops that I had to visit. As I headed through the 3rd floor God reminded me that I needed to buy some pyjamas for M.

I stood with my purchases at the cash register and waited. An older lady called J was all anxious etc. Her credit card would not work – I wanted to get home, but chose to remain calm and I offered to pay for her goods. She accepted and then told me about her grandkids and started to cry. I said to wait and I would pray for her.

She waited as I paid for my purchase and we stood to the side and prayed. She wept under the anointing.

She then started to pour her heart some more. I bought her a hot chocolate and listened while she told me her story in the middle of Myers and offered to pray some more. She had arthritis – I held her hand, commanded the arthritis to go, and then felt to take her to her 'God space'.

When she had located her God space she said God was 'way up in Heaven' and she was 'down here with me' (we were still sitting in Myer). I said, 'ask Him to come closer'. She did. I asked her where He was. She said on the couch opposite us. I said, 'do you want Him to come closer?' – she said 'yes'.

I said, 'ask Him to come closer'; she did, and started to cry. The anointing grew heavy. I asked where He was and she said He was kneeling right in front of her and that He was saying that He had forgiven her. I told her to tell Him what she wanted to tell Him – she wept and said sorry for being away from Him.

I then felt to say, 'would you like to ask Him into your heart'. She said she had a long time ago, but I said, 'do you want to ask Him again, afresh' – she said 'yes'. She recommitted her life to Him and shook and wept as he started to heal her broken heart. The anointing was very strong and thick – it grew stronger and stronger each time she asked Him to come closer and closer – I shook a bit and could feel Him all over us. She could feel tingling on/in her hands. We talked some more and she asked Holy Spirit to come and wash her clean, and back into her heart.

After she had recommitted her life to Jesus Christ I prayed and told the demonic to go and not come back, and for Holy Spirit to fill her completely up. I also prayed an impartation of the gift of healing after she said she wanted it.

Office healing...

A lovely elderly gentleman in our office had a quadruple bypass last year. This winter season he has been struggling with a chest infection that just won't seem to heal. He said it was related to his operation last year when they had deflated his lungs during the operation. So I asked him if he believed in God to which he replied yes, he was Greek Orthodox. I explained to him that I have been challenged by the scripture in Mark 16:17-18 where it says: 'And these signs will accompany those who have believed: in my name.... they will lay hands on the sick and they will recover' I either believe or I don't and if I do, then I have to activate it.

So I asked if I could lay hands on his chest and pray for him. At which he replied yes, that would be good. (He's Greek, so imagine the heavy Greek accent!) I then thanked God for this gentle man that has such an amazing heart for his family and others. I then commanded the infection to go in Jesus' name. I then felt compelled to pray healing, favour and blessing over him and his family. He thanked me very much when I had finished and we went back to work. That afternoon he took the time out to come downstairs and thank me again and said he was going to claim the blessings!

Yesterday he reported to me that he saw his doctor on Monday who was astonished to see that there was no more infection in his lungs! Praise God! and Yay God!

A young lady blesses and is blessed...

This is what happened for the people I prayed for. The first person that I did was Maddy and she had left ankle problems and so we prayed for her and then she felt a warm and fuzzy feeling and she felt a little bit better.

What happened to Maddy was the same as what happened to another girl but with her back. There was this other lady who had about a 6 or 7 pain out of 10 and when we prayed for her, her ankle felt about 3 or 4 and so we did it again and she ended up being like a 1 and so we prayed once more and she only had ¼ out of 10 pain then. There was another lady who had a very bad problem with her ankle and she had the pain for about 6 to 12 years and the doctors had been trying to work out what's wrong and trying to make it better, and so we prayed for her a couple of times and she didn't feel any pain and there was another two ladies who had been needing some encouragement but they haven't had much, mostly they had just had discouragement. We prayed for them and they felt really good and one of the girls wanted to give me a hug and I said yes they could.

There was this man who came up and he needed some encouragement too, because he had been sick and the doctors gave him some drugs to help him get better and he got addicted to them. He just needed some prayer so he could get off them and so we did and he felt God a lot and fell down, not like he fell down by accident. It was God.

It was a bit scary to pray for the first person but after a while I got the hang of it and I didn't know if they heard me or not but I just kept praying.

THEN on Sunday night when Jen and Brian were at church singing, I was lying next to mum, soaking. Mum told me that there had been feathers falling and I lay down and I was talking to God and listening to the music. I felt like I was in a cradle with God rocking me to help me go to sleep, and I started to feel like I was the baby being rocked and I woke up and God picked me up and made me feel better. I also heard angels singing during worship and this other lady also said she heard angels as well.

While I was on the carpet I was praying for feathers and I didn't know it but mum had also been praying for feathers for me. The next morning I found really, really, really fluffy white feathers on my rug like the ones that were falling at church! I know God gave me feathers because He can and to let us know that He is there and the His is real and listens to us when we are talking to Him.

Young believers jump on board...

R and I went to the supermarket. While collecting the groceries I saw in the corner of my eye a lady shoplifting. I questioned why did God allow me to see that, what am I supposed to do with that information. I wandered through the supermarket asking for guidance, asking God to help me make the right decision.

Going through the register the same lady was in front of me, she was very thin and had the appearance and energy of someone who was struggling with life. Her grocery items came to a total of around $75. She opened her wallet to pay. I stepped forward (R was thinking 'what are you doing D?', but did not say a word). I looked at the lady and said 'I do not want you to get into trouble, but I saw what you did'. I asked her to return the goods onto the counter and I would pay for her shopping. She reached into her top and pulled out the stolen item (a big block of cheese). Her eyes filled up as she told me it was survival that made her do it and she didn't really want to and felt terrible. I paid for her shopping. We then stepped to the side and held hands and prayed, she looked me in the eyes and said, 'you have my word I will never, ever, ever do that again'. She raised her arms in the air and wept as God touched her heart. R and I left the supermarket, got in the car and felt that 'too drunk to drive' feeling. We sat quietly and thanked the Lord for creating the unspoken mutual understanding that R and I both have, that will allow us to step forward and help others, knowing that I have R's full support and vice versa – that he has mine.

Following the Spirit's prompts...

I went to the skate park with the kids while my husband was playing cricket at the same park. Three kids came to play there too. I was listening to a podcast about awakening and I felt prompted to talk to these kids about Jesus.

To cut a long story short, three kids aged 9, 10 and 16 gave their hearts to the Lord. One was a re-dedication – a 16 year old from South Africa (went to church in South Africa that had three stories, it was so big!) and the other two were first timers. K [the writer's 5 year old daughter] was talking to the 3 year old's dad just a few feet away when the boy came crying to his dad. K asked if she could pray and they said 'yes'. The little boy felt better!

I must say, I had an attitude about going to a skate park and have been stalling this decision for months.

God's timing is perfect. The kids who got saved, their dads were also playing cricket and they were just hanging around!! But not in God's eyes. It was a divine appointment... and my kids had the best time ever!! So did I!!

Anytime, anywhere...

I drove to the DFO and felt to go to a shop opposite. I was not sure why, but as we wandered I saw a woman with a wrist brace on – she had torn tendons in her wrist and thumb. I offered to pray. She agreed and she told me she felt tingling... which continued after I finished as she continued around the store.

Another woman saw me further around the store and said something about the stress she was feeling – she was hosting her son's wedding reception at her home and Christmas. I agreed that **would** be stressful. She said thank you – I felt I had somehow **seen** her.

I came across her again. I felt she had been watching me and was placing herself in my path. She engaged me in further conversation during which I asked her if she would like me to pray for her. She readily agreed saying she saw me over the other side praying for the other woman... 'she **had** been watching me', I thought, and she wanted prayer.

Her name was Joy. Well I prayed for Joy... for Joy to be released into her destiny, and for joy (the Spirit of Joy) to come upon and within her... for her to receive joy, and to **be** Joy and all that entailed... I also prayed into the other circumstances she had shared with me... all the while my 3-year old was wandering...

As I prayed I looked at her and said 'you can feel that can't you?' She nodded and nearly started crying. Whin I finished, she looked and me and said she wondered if I knew some Christians on her street in a nearby suburb.

I thought, 'Oh no... here we go', but then she told me their names and there were my pastors! She said I was just like them... she had been watching them, and now she had been watching me. God was obviously on her case. My pastor's witness had impacted her, and it was no co-incidence that I had come and prayed for her. I told her that I had not known why I had come to the shop, but it was apparently for her... it was not a coincidence, God **was** on her case.

I wished her well and finished wandering through the shop.

Suffice to say, my barrel was empty today. Like many people at this time of year, life is busy, children excited and their behaviour can be challenging, people make demands and others can be unkind, we can **feel** our barrel empty... we have nothing of ourselves to give however... God's barrel is never empty... despite me and my circumstances as I reached into my empty barrel, God came through and touched three thirsty women all in the space of about an hour. All needed a touch of God for different reasons...

As long as I will stop for the one, regardless of how I **feel**, regardless of me my God can and does move to touch a hurting world, and today I saw how His arm **is** long enough to embrace others, His grace **is** sufficient for my needs and His desires to be fulfilled. His barrel **is** deep enough and His power **is** ever available... **despite me...** if I will only stop for the one... and allow the river to flow, not only will He refresh me as He flows **through** me, but He will also show the world that God is good!

Testimony of Jesus impacts MS...

I was at a family gathering and a lady was sharing about how her sister was in a wheelchair and had MS. She also shared that her nephew (her brother's son) had been in a wheelchair after having a virus that attacked his muscles. He is only 19! The day before I had been at a women's conference and had seen many people healed and compassion rose up in me when I heard her speak about her family. This family are all Roman Catholic and have grown up to love God but had no experience of His healing power.

I took her aside because I had to tell her about the healing power of Jesus. When I began to speak her eyes lit up and she said 'I have never heard of this before, but I believe it'. Tears began to well up in her eyes, and immediately she said 'Would you come and pray for my sister?'. I think the thing that struck me the most was that I have a harder time convincing Christians that Jesus can heal, and this person who has no experience of the supernatural power of God was ready to receive. She said to me 'I never knew this could happen – no-one had ever told me this before!'

When I went to her house she had invited a lot of her family there. lol! There were about seven of them. They had made pizzas and gone to so much effort. They were ready to receive – it was a very big occasion for them! We chatted for a bit. They asked a lot of questions about healing and I shared testimonies from Bethel and from our church. Then they said 'Can we stop talking and can you just pray!' HA HA!

So I laid my hand on the lady in the wheelchair. As we began to pray God's presence came into the room. She jolted in her chair twice and said to me 'Can you fell that?' I said that I could. She felt an electric shock go through her body twice and then she felt heat go through her legs. 'Normally my legs feel cold and like lead, but I can feel heat', she said. So I said to her, 'Is there anything you could not do before that you could try doing now?' She said she had not stood up for a very long time – around seven years. So I told her to get out of the wheelchair.

She stood up with all of us holding her. She then wriggled her legs around. It was so awesome. Then she sat down again and talked with me some more. Then we got her up again and she stood again. Then I prayed for her whole family and prophesied and sang over them. It was so wonderful to see this family loving Jesus and ready to receive from Him. I also prayed over the nephew who had been in a wheelchair but was still quite sick. It seemed to me that there was some sort of generational curse and I prayed against that, and shared with them that I felt this was the case.

As I as about to leave, the lady in the wheelchair told me she still felt heat in her legs. I believe she will be totally healed. Then they wanted to know if there was anywhere they could go to learn about Jesus and His healing power. Of course I invited them to church.

I was so humbled by this experience because I almost did not go to pray for her as I was not feeling so well myself. What I have learned is that it really is not about us. It's not about how we feel. Just believe Him and pray. It's as simple as that. I feel the Lord has been saying to me lately 'Your job is to pray for people. My job is to heal. So you just do your bit and don't worry about the healing bit – that's My job.'

Identity, destiny and salvation...

Last Friday night felt very much like the end of something... it felt like the end of term, even though it was only a mid-term break for our 8-year old's school. With that feeling, I had the sense that we were to have dinner out... I was quite happy to have it at home, but there was this feeling that we were to eat out and it felt like a place down on the beach, close to where we live.

I called my husband and he agreed so we booked a table as the heavens opened and the torrential rains came...

We ran into the establishment through the rain and there was a beautiful young blond girl who met us at the door. I laughed at my dishevelled look, and mentioned to the girl that we had left a message. She replied that the storm had stopped all calls coming in and out and that she had not received the messages... she **was** stressed. I motioned to the storm outside and mentioned my dishevelled look, laughing at the frizz and curls, she readily agreed saying she had stood under the hand dryer for ages, trying to dry **her** hair into some semblance of order... I told her she looked absolutely gorgeous (she really did) and she seemed to relax somewhat, smiling as she got us our menus and glasses of water... and laughing as our 4-year-old said something funny... As we talked and laughed as a family, I sensed that God had a word for someone, and as I questioned it I sensed that it was for the beautiful girl who had first served us. I got the serviette, found a pen and started to write the word I got. It included that she had a gift for making people comfortable, but that was not all she was created for, it said that God wanted her comfortable too... for He loved her and created her for greatness...

I sensed she was artistic in what she did, that she needed to step into her destiny and it had something to do with being artistic, and I thought 'oh no not a destiny word' and felt somewhat intimidated about stepping out and prophesying it... what if I got it all wrong about her?

We ate out meals and as we were about to leave I saw where she was in the room and went over to her with my serviette.

I explained that I was a Christian and that sometimes I felt got 'words' from God for people, and I asked her if I could share what I felt I had heard about her...

She agreed and so I started to read...

As I read she nodded, and then I got to the destiny bit and I took a deep breath and said that the next bit frightened me a bit to say, but that I would read it and she could tell me what she felt about it... I then went on to say I felt she was artistic and that it was time for her to step out

194

into what she was called to do... she was artistic and creative... I stopped and asked her whether any of it made sense to her and tears were in her eyes...She went on to explain that her entire family were artistic, but she had never seen herself that way... but that she hated what she was doing, and was considering stepping out and doing interior design... and as she spoke I looked at her and said what came to me, as a knowing filled me for her and her circumstances...

I said to her, 'you have been comparing yourself to your family. You think you do not measure up. You think you are not artistic, because of how remarkable they are, but oh, you are artistic, you were created to be artistic, you were created for greatness and I sense that God is saying no more comparison, no more comparing yourself to others, for you are created as an original and you were created to shine...' and the word went on and on about her God-given artistic ability and that the pathway was before her that she just needed to step out into with courage...

As I spoke into her destiny, tears filled her eyes... I then asked if I could pray for her, quickly telling her the testimony of an open destiny for one of my friend's husbands (see below for links to testimonies) and she said 'yes' and so I prayed and declared her destiny open, I rebuked the lies of doubt, closed the past and released her into the fullness of who she was called to be... and the tears glistened as she dabbed at her eyes, and her eyes locked onto mine, with me trusting that she would see only God, not me, and hear the truth of all I was declaring over her...

I then sensed God say to ask her if she wanted to ask Jesus into her heart... so I did...

She said she had been raised a Catholic. I said, 'you have never asked Him into your heart have you?'... she hadn't and wanted to and so I led her in a very simple prayer of salvation. She then asked Holy Spirit to fill her up. I asked if I could hug her, and as she nodded, I wrapped my arms around her and exclaimed how incredibly special she truly was...I then felt Holy Spirit say... 'that's it' so I said my goodbyes looking back at her as she stood in the dining room...

I wanted to fix it all for her, be her encourager, be there for her in the journey, but my part, for now, was over... it was the end of something, it was the end of the lies and deception that she had believed for so long, and it was the beginning of something new and amazing...

I saw a beautiful young girl full of promise, touched and filled by a great God, a loving God, an all-knowing God, a God who wanted her to see herself the way that He saw her... she had been touched by a God that loved her so very much that He sent us down there as a family to have dinner so He could let her know the truth about herself, so she could be released into a destiny she was born for because...

God is good!

Healed in the presence of God...

Two weeks ago during praise and worship in church Sunday service, something incredible happened to me. Just some background story for u guys. I had injuries twice on my left knee few years ago, and the condition was quite bad that I put too much strain on my right leg for support which then cause both legs to be very weak over the years. Normally during worship in church, I won't be able to stand through the whole session due to intense pain all the way to my toes. It's just impossible for me to keep standing for too long.

So what happened that morning was I was so overwhelmed by God's presence during worship in church that I didn't realise I actually stood for quite long already. Before worship ended a guy went up to share about his vision on stage, and suddenly there was this voice in me that said, 'Hey, look! You're still standing!' I was shocked, of course, and looked at both my knees, literally – no pain and my legs were so light! It's indescribable. I thought I could fly. XD

I kinda doubt that healing just happened to me. When I sat down I crossed my legs and kept changing sides to check if the pain ever comes back again (coz normally if i cross my legs it gets really painful too). But

196

no, Totally NO PAIN. I've never experienced such feeling for almost seven years.

When I came back from church, my housemate and I were trying to change the light globes on the ceiling. I climbed up and down the table, chair and bed for around ten times and again, NEVER ONCE DID I FEEL ANY PAIN ON BOTH KNEES. TOTALLY PAIN-FREE, and STABILITY like never before. Now that is really quite something because if I ever tell my parents I did that with those (old) knees they would kill me. But no, not anymore, coz I was assured that I just got HEALED BY OUR ALMIGHTY GOD!!!!

For the whole day God reminded me about the verse I was meditating on last night '...where the spirit of the Lord is, there is freedom'. This year in my uni OCF we're focusing on pursuing the presence of God, and that morning in church I could feel His presence so strong in our midst and FUHHH, I was set free of the pain I've been experiencing for almost seven years now.

It was just another ordinary morning in church and nobody laid hands on me and I wasn't even thinking about healing for my knees but when we worshipped and the presence of God came, heaven invaded earth and I got what I, as God's daughter, deserve - HEALING, MIRACLE and the HEAVENLY JOY. It's just as simple as that. Healing doesn't only come during conference/crusade. God's ready to heal anytime, anywhere.

It kept me thinking, if only we could dwell in His presence every day and night, miracles and healing can be just another norm of our daily lives. How awesome is that :) I'm thirsting for more, seriously. :)

EVERY ATTEMPT IS A SUCCESS

In Chapter One I noted the importance of a permission-giving culture that empowers people with the truth that 'every attempt is a success'. We have learned to celebrate the attempt as much as we celebrate the outcome. Here are some stories to illustrate how our congregation are stepping up and into the normal Christian life.

Adding healing to a shopping list...

Just an aside – had to pop up to Coles this morning for milk for the office. As I parked, a kind man moved a trolley so that I could get into the park. As I got out I thanked him and noticed he was hobbling (he was quite old and had a walking stick), so I asked him why he was hobbling and he shared with me that he'd had a hip operation and while resting at home, his wife had fallen and as he hopped up to help her he didn't get his leg out of the way fast enough and broke his thigh bone. He now has a metal plate and screws in it. Jokingly he told me that next time he goes to the airport it will be funny because the metal detectors will go crazy. As we chatted I casually asked him if I could pray for him, because I believed that Jesus would like to see him healed; he agreed, he bowed his head and I prayed, asking the Holy Spirit to come and for healing and restoration in his leg and just for good measure a miracle that all of the metal would disappear. I thank God for this lovely man S, who was so positive with a good sense of humour.

Nothing dramatic happened there and then, but he thanked me and was tickled that someone cared enough to stop and chat. I went my way to buy my milk for the office all the while continuing to pray favour and blessing over him and his wife.

Such a good feeling to know you have put a smile on someone's face just by stopping for the one. I trust God to take care of him, I may never know the end result but I'm pretty confident it will be spectacular!

Age is no barrier...

We went to a shopping centre on Wednesday night and saw a boy with a broken toe. I asked my three year old if she would like to offer to pray for him. As we got to the point of praying, my five year old stepped up and commanded the pain to leave, with my five year old repeating what she prayed as she prayed it. It was hilarious. I asked the boy if he felt any better and he said it does feel a bit better actually. He was very grateful.

So, we keep taking about it to them and telling them how amazing they are... it has taken a few years of them seeing this, but I am so happy I feel like they just got it this week.

Sharing faith...

On a very fun note and for the joys of sharing, this morning I had a chiro appointment. I sat in my car umming and ah-ing whether to read a magazine in the waiting room or my bible (The Message). Eventually decided I'd take my bible in. So I read my bible while I waited. My time comes. I put my bible down on the floor and bag on top, and the chiro begun his work. He's working on my neck when he sees my bible and asks 'are you reading the New Testament?', I reply 'arrr yes.' He goes on to share that he had just started reading it, he's up to John... and the conversation goes on about God and our experiences etc. The best part about the experiences was; this year I've had many medical appointments and have found myself double-guessing Jesus and His power in the waiting rooms. I've wanted so badly to love these people that look oppressed and see them experience the joy of a touch of God (using the ill health as a path way in) but fearful about the potential question of 'if you believe He heals so strongly why are you here?' or 'why are you not healed?' I began wondering how do I do this, how can it be possible, and today God showed me that again, I just have to be me (He is inside very ready to express Himself outwardly) and that it is very possible!

At a child's birthday party

Last Saturday I attended a Healing Workshop. During the first session 'healing for pelvis' was released and so I stood and laid hands on myself – I had been diagnosed with pelvic instability (very rare) during my two pregnancies.

After the sessions, having thoroughly enjoyed the workshops and feeling refreshed from being in the tangible presence of God... having received impartation, I went to collect my nearly five-year-old son from a birthday party. While saying our goodbyes a girl I barely knew from the kindy came and spoke to me, showing me her new one-week-old baby boy... As we chatted she mentioned that she had been struggling with pelvic instability... not an extreme case but, nonetheless, nasty!

I thought 'No coincidence!'...

I had been set up again... for her...

So often we receive impartation and then it's time to step out and give away what we have received... and if we do... it WILL increase... so we have more to give away... and more to give away... and so on and so on...

I had stood to receive pelvic healing for myself (I am healed, but occasionally it would twinge), when in fact God was releasing it upon me for others... I was to give it away...

I offered to pray, explaining I had suffered the same condition. To my surprise she agreed... and so I stood in the driveway with people milling around, laid my hands on her hips and prayed, releasing healing in the name of Jesus. She felt warmth. I suggested she take note of any improvement, no matter how slight, and to thank God for it... She agreed she would...I am looking forward to seeing her after the summer holidays... in February when our school and kindy go back...

Our kids can lead the way...

We have had two very exciting Sundays.

A fortnight ago the group created Prophetic Art to give to members of the congregation via placing it on their car windscreens. I have had really good feedback on this with a number of people reporting back to Roselyn that the words and pictures that were in the cards were incredibly meaningful and encouraging.

Last Weekend, we went a step further and created prophetic art for people at Forest Hill Chase. We had a group of eighteen kids. They heard from God, and very quickly made a card, and also filled out a sheet with a description of who they should find to give the card to.

Once we were at Forest Hill Chase, the time went very quickly. We broke up into five groups, and proceeded to put on our 'Jesus eyes' and locate the recipients of the cards.

My group of three boys quickly found two men that matched the descriptions that the boys had listed. The first gentleman was surprised by the approach of the young person, and received the card as well as listened to what other thoughts that God had given. I then asked if he wanted us to pray a blessing over his life, which he politely declined.

The next gentleman was similar in response, but the exciting part was seeing how bold the boys were in approaching someone. They were very pumped!

The last card was to be given to a lady in a red top. The card was a picture of a sunrise, and the theme was Joy, Peace, and encouragement. We found this lady with a group of people sitting in the food court. This time C approached the lady and shared the words that God had given him. The group and the lady were really amazed. They had just come from a Church service which was very sad, one of the prominent members of the Church had passed away last week, and that morning the minister had announced that he was resigning from service. The Lady (and the group of friends) felt very encouraged. In the excitement, we forgot to ask whether we could pray for them!

After this our group wandered around looking for other people that we could give prophetic words to - that was fun.

One of the Activate girls [Grades 5 and 6] had a very specific list of identifying characteristics. Things like, teenager wearing jeans, white top, specific shoes, and a first name. It was not until almost the end of time at the shopping centre that they found someone matching the description. The teenage girl was really encouraged to receive the card, and also enjoyed being prayed for.

One of the kids had a description of a lady who was a mum-to-be (pregnant), with specific coloured hair, and clothes. M was with the girls, and they found this lady with her partner and small child. They explained that they were on a Treasure Hunt and God had showed them what to put in the card. The lady read the card, and then started crying. She shared that they had been recently told that the baby in the womb was sick. The family allowed the girls to pray for them. They felt really encouraged.

Out of the 18 cards - 14 found a person that matched the description or clues. All of the kids said they would love to do that again. None of them wanted to go back to Church - they were having so much fun!

Releasing peace...

About three or four weeks ago someone had given me a picture that he felt God was showing for me. It was a picture of shoes with the word 'peace' on them. Not knowing exactly what that meant, I stored it away in the back of my mind, but the events of this day seem pertinent to that picture...

I had an incredible opportunity the other day to pray for my hairdresser. Her business closed down about a year ago but she kept some of her clients... she comes to our house to do our hair.

While she was cutting my hair this time she began sharing about the incredible mess some of her family relationships are in at the moment. We talked about that for a while and then went on to other general topics. As I was cleaning up from the haircut I said to her: 'Just as you were sharing some of those things earlier about what's going on for you at home, I felt that God wanted me to offer to pray for you.' I quickly added 'you can have whatever response you want, but I just felt to ask'. I was anticipating that she would feel really awkward about it, but she teared up and said that she would be open to almost anything at the moment. My Mum was also having her hair cut so we decided to pray after Mum's haircut.

While Mum was having her haircut I was Skyping with a friend overseas. While I Skyped I offered to pray for her Grandma who has gone into a nursing home and has been quite angry with the nursing staff. I prayed what I felt to pray – for a release of God's peace in her nursing home room.

Mum's haircut was finished, and she invited our hairdresser to stay for lunch. She was quite chatty and even after we'd finished eating she wasn't rushing off to leave. During a pause in the conversation I asked if she still wanted me to pray... I had given her so many opportunities to back out!

She said 'yes' so I put my hand on her shoulder and specifically prayed for peace in her heart and in her relationships, and that she would be very aware of God's presence as she went back to her home. I didn't feel anything, just a strong sense to pray for peace. As I finished she looked up and said 'I feel really relaxed now!', and went on to say that whenever she comes to our home it doesn't feel like work for her to cut our hair, that she feels peace when she comes here, and she looks forward to these times.

As soon as she left I did a little dance.

Go God! He's so amazing.

I'm excited to see what will happen in my hairdresser's journey.

Crossing the chicken line...

Our journey has been facilitated and catalysed by a number of people from outside our congregation. One of those is Kevin Dedmon. Along with his son Chad, Kevin inspired our young adult community to 'cross the chicken line'. That is, most of us face a 'fear barrier' when it comes to asking others if we can pray for them; or, offering to do something kind; or, to share our faith; or to respond to an unusual prompt form the Holy Spirit. This 'fear barrier' is our own personal 'chicken line' that needs to be crossed to live a normal Christian life of having heaven invade earth through us. Here are some of the stories posted on our Stairway young adult community Facebook group.

At the railway station...

Hey so I finally have a chicken line story – even though it was kinda forced by J, but I maintain it still counts.

So J in our connect group has decided to give us money each week so that we can bless someone with it. She was really sneaky and didn't tell us, she just put the money in the middle and waited for someone to pick it up. This is when E picked it up and gave it to me!! So I was stuck with having to do something nice to someone, and I had till next connect group to do it.

I know I'm a really confident person, but this stuff FREAKS ME OUT. I started praying about who God wanted me to do something for, but nothing really came. Anyway over the next few weeks I kept seeing people at the station on the way to Uni looking through bins for tickets. I had NEVER seen it but it kept happening!! This was obviously my cue, so I went to the station a bit earlier on the way to Uni, determined to give someone money for a train ticket. I saw one lady, and she was really highlighted to me, she even stopped right in front of me but I completely chickened out and went on my train. My two weeks was up, and I decided I had to face my fears and get over it. I was with H at the time and we waited at the station together. I decided I wasn't going to go up to someone, but really prayed that I would see someone looking for a ticket in the bin. We waited for about 10 minutes and didn't see anyone. I was about to give up when I saw this older Chinese lady walking around aimlessly. I was really hesitant about going up to her, firstly because I was afraid she couldn't speak English, and second because what if she actually wasn't looking for a ticket. Then it happened, I saw her looking around for used tickets and realised this is who it was meant for! I was about to chicken out again (thank God H was with me), and she pushed me to go up to her. So I DID IT. I went over to her and explained that I noticed she was looking for a train ticket and I wanted to give her money to pay for one. She was SHOCKED. She tried to give the money back at first, asking 'Why me'. When I said I wanted to bless her 'just because', her face just lit up! She thanked me and I just wished her a good day and left.

This was such a big step for me! I am so, so, so, so, so scared of rejection and looking like an idiot that I decided I wasn't going to do anything like that. Like, I'm always up for helping people, but the second it starts getting scary I'll just think - 'Someone else can do it'. But doing that made me realise that I'M THE SOMEONE. But it's crazy how abandoning all those fears just to make someone's day really pays off.

So thank you to J, E and H for pushing me to actually step out there. And I know this is a super long post (but it's impossible for me NOT to write heaps), and I really wanna encourage you to push past your fears, no matter how YOU are feeling, and make someone's day. It's seriously epic.

Lack of interest is no barrier...

Hey guys. Some of you may have seen this on a private post on my own page but thought it might be of encouragement here too:

So. Turned up to Stairway church last Sunday night and was invited by T to go out during the service and demonstrate what was going to be preached about: taking God's love to people on the street. Why not! My middle name is risk!

Went to Brentford Square. Had some really interesting encounters like meeting a man whose son had just died fighting in Afghanistan (which you can probably hear about on the Stairway podcast). One story we didn't get to mention to the church when we came back:

As we were getting ready to leave T was telling me how it was a shame we hadn't seen anybody with an obvious physical ailment 'cos it can be easier approaching them when you know there is something you can offer to pray for. Then this lady hobbles past and I was like, 'Well T, there's your obvious physical symptom'. So we approached the lady in the supermarket and she told us she had problems from head to toe but wasn't interested in prayer – she'd 'been there, done that.' But there was another lady just next to us paying for her groceries who had been eavesdropping on us and she started talking to us: turns out some other people from Stairway had approached her and a girl that was with her (I think it was her daughter) at Forest Hill shopping centre just the week before (what are the chances?!). And these Stairway people had prayed for the girl who had some serious eye problem (can't remember what it was now). And this lady just wanted to let me and T know that the girl's eye had been completely healed. Then we prayed for the lady who was now ill herself, and T started to notice a change in the lady's condition and felt to let the lady know that she would be feeling better by the time she got home from the shops. So there you go: well worth going after the hobbling lady who wasn't interested in prayer.

God has a master plan and we all get to be a part of it. Even if you're like me and have no idea what the plan is most of the time – God honours the desire to be part of it. Doesn't have to be approaching people on the street – whatever your gifting/passion is.

Now, that's unusual...

Here's another one for the collection of chicken stories... even if you're too nervous to go and 'evangelise' face to face, sometimes, you don't even have to go anywhere to look for people who need to hear about how much God loves them... they come to you!!! Let me explain – I'm sure since it's me, an explanation is always mandatory :-)

One of the delightful thirty-two youngsters I've fostered in the last 6 yrs decided it'd be a good giggle to write my phone number and the phrase, 'Call me' next to it, on the back of a seat on a bus. Today, I get two random sms's from peeps, but just figure they've somehow got the wrong number. But then I got to thinking, 'Hang on, here's an opportunity to connect with these people, not in a '1300' sort of way :-) So, sms conversations went back and forth, got talking to a gorgeous teenage girl who was riding that particular bus with her boyfriend at the time, and was basically able to sms the Gospel to her, and say that I don't think ANYTHING happens without good reason. She wasn't even sure what made her send a txt in the first place!! Got some words of knowledge for her, shared them, freaked her out a bit, cos they were spot-on, prophesied over her, and ooop dere dis! Go God! (via rebellious foster kids who He loves just as much as the peeps who read my number on the seat :-P)

Caring for the popular...

Got a chicken line story for ya!

So a couple of weeks ago I read in the Sunday paper about Brooke Hanson (the swimmer) losing her nine-month old baby boy. It broke my heart and I cried for a long time, totally touched by her pain. At the time I really felt like I was meant to get Chris Pringle's book about losing her son, Jesse, (**Jesse: Found in Heaven**) to Brooke somehow and to let her know that God was crying with her for her loss. Anyway, today I was sitting in Barclays cafe and who should walk in and SIT RIGHT NEXT TO ME but Brooke Hanson and her hubby! I immediately knew God was asking me to speak to her and bless her, but I totally vowed that I was not, under any circumstances, going to invade her privacy in a public place... Well, God had other plans! My heart thumped so loud that I thought everyone could hear. Then Brooke kept on turning around and smiling at me, checking out the menu above my head, making eye contact.... Far out! God made it sooooo hard for me to ignore His prompting!!! Eventually I just decided to get up and leave! But as I stood up, she smiled again and I knew God had suckered me! Nevertheless, I still tried to leave without speaking to her, but as I left the cafe, I found myself walking into the florist next door, buying a bunch of yellow roses and a card and giving them to Brooke with an explanation that God wanted to bless her and a note about Chris's book included. She thanked me and said with tears flowing that I'd made her day and gave me a big hug. I realized then that I was such a twit for even trying to bail out of God's plan, because all He's interested in is dishing out love and my silly ideas just slow down that process! God, you totally rock and thanks for being patient with me!

God and crime...

Well, apparently I've found a new way to cross the chicken line and I didn't even have to talk to anyone face to face! Ha!

Here's the story – it started yesterday. I was on the eastern freeway driving along and saw a motorbike on the opposite side of the road (it was parked on the shoulder with no one with it). I had this funny thought, 'what if you could give a word for the person who owns that and leave it for them on their bike, for when they get back).' As I thought about it longer I imagined what I'd say if I wrote a to them... as I did this I felt a word of knowledge come into my head... and BAM I got off at the next exit and turned around. I put my hazards on and parked behind the bike. I wrote a note to the mystery biker it started off something like: 'If you are reading this note I am presuming you have either stolen or own this bike' ha! Anyway I went on to say, not sure if you believe in this sorta thing but I felt like Jesus showed me something about you, so I thought I'd write you this note. The word was about this person being a real light to the people in their world, and someone who gives clarity and understanding to situations, and that they needed to know this because at times they may have felt like giving up, but that they shouldn't because they're doing a really great job. Anyway, I left it on the bike with a sign saying please read, and my number if they wanted to get in touch (I wonder what will happen)...

So today I get a text from a random who reported the bike to the police. Turns out the bike was stolen. The police had found the owner and were returning the bike and MY NOTE! ha, so this guy read it and the police. And the guy was just telling me he read it but was passing it on.etc. Anyway random, nothing much came of that, until at 6pm tonight... I get a call from C. He's my mystery bikey! ha. He was a young guy and he said he got the note. I said I was sorry about his bike being stolen, he seemed fine about it. But basically he said what I wrote in the note was 'spot on' and that he did feel like a light in situations etc.. He asked if I was religious I said yes and that I believe in Jesus and I'm a Christian. He said it was good to know there was 'someone upstairs looking out for us'... I said yep, and told him it was nice to speak to him. And that was about it! HA! I love my own story... it's so creative! For all you shy peeps out there, totally try a note!!! HA

In the drive-thru...

YES!!! A poultry-line story over Easter! Needed to get cash out for M, so went through drive-thru and ordered a soft drink and then asked for cash out. That was all fine. The girl that did the transaction at the first window looked a little stressed out. Then I stopped guessing stuff about her and God started talking. He told me to go and withdraw a very specific amount of money. (for which I had to go and find an ATM belonging to the bank I'm with, therefore defeating the purpose of 'convenient drive-thru cash!!) I did this, told M what was going on, and funnily enough, she barely even blinked. I think she's used to her odd mum by now!! So back we go, and I'm running all these rehearsed lines through my head bout how I'm going to explain this to the girl. Anyway, again, I stop practising... and ask God how HE wants me to play it. As I put the money into an envelope I had in the car, He says, 'Just share with her that you believe in Me.' Um, OK, that seems a little ambiguous and vague, but what the heck, who am I to argue with the Creator of the Universe??

So I pulled up to her window again at the drive-thru, and bear in mind it's stupid o-clock in the morning, around 1am maybe. I say what God told me to say, and that I'm a Christian. She looks at me and says really quickly, 'Yeah! So am I.' So I told her that the next bit should be really easy for her to receive then, and even easier for me to explain! 'God told me to give you this amount of money. No idea what it's about, but there you go. Here it is.' She hesitates to take it, until I remind her that given I've never met her before, I'm sure it's from God! She takes it, opens it, and right there, at the drive-thru window inside the store, she starts shaking and crying. It's an amount she's needed to pay a phone bill that's been stressing her out recently. She said she's currently at university, got a ridiculous bill for her mobile as she'd unknowingly gone over her new phone cap, was now working double shifts, and was contemplating dropping out of studies cos she wasn't sure how she was going to find the money she needed for bills, uni, mortgage, etc. and was just feeling really overwhelmed. At that, I felt I just really needed to state the obvious, and said, 'Well, it looks like God's given you your answer as to where all that money's going to come from, take care, God bless.' That was it. :-)

Even when it should be safe...

So, God did a pretty cool thing last night at our small group. J told me that she was struggling with a bad migraine, had it all day and couldn't concentrate. I thought, well, let's pray for you in the midst of worship. Some of you may or may not know, but God has been talking to me for a while about recording pieces of music for people's healing in certain areas. I've started on a few but have been found myself getting increasingly frustrated because I know that just an old strum on the guitar isn't what he requires. He requires me to be so engaged with him, so in his presence that as he breathes into me, it comes out in the form of an instrumental. L has been having increased amounts of migraines and he has been the one that I've been focusing on lately, trying to record a song that reverses the effects of the migraine, and fills his mind with a concentrated dose of his presence. As I've sat down to record things, nothing has felt totally right... So last night as we were worshipping, a melody dropped into the top of my head and I just started playing it, very gently. I then said to J, 'I feel like God just gave me this melody to counterattack your migraine right now. And as I play I just want you to focus on him (the solution) and not the migraine (the problem). What God gave me to play, sounded like clockwork. Very simple, very rhythmic, very persistent. I then said ' I feel like this melody represents how the mind works. In sync, in time, and ongoing. I feel that right now he's started to rewind the effects of your migraine and He's resetting your mind's clock to how he wants it to run... As the melody played, his anointing filled the room and J started laughing and shaking her head... She said 'I can't believe this, but I can, but I can't. The migraine felt like it just rewound out the front of my head, towards the back and just left.' We all gave thanks and celebrated together.

Guys, crossing your chicken line may not look like everyone else's. It doesn't have to. Your an individual creation and different from the next. Crossing 'your' chicken line could be painting a picture and handing it to someone, it could be writing a poem about someone that depicts how God sees them. Let's not limit ourselves, and most of all not limit God, but constantly be in a conversation with him on how 'he' wants to cross our chicken line :)

KIDS JUMPING ON BOARD

There are so many stunning outcomes arising out of the journey we are on. One of those is the way our children have so readily embraced the possibilities. While I have already provided some of the kids' stories, some more will be good. We need to be reminded that they are not filled with and led by a 'junior' Holy Spirit!

Beloved toy returns...

I was four when this happened and it starts at church. Mum was doing the tithe. Then she held up a $100 note. Mum said 'who wants this $100 note? People put up their hand. Mum said 'I will give it to whoever asks for it and comes to take it.' No-one came forward, no-one moved. She said 'who wants this? I really will give it to who ever asks.' No-one moved or asked, but me. I walked towards her in front of everyone and said,' I will, I'll have it' and I put my hand up for it. So mum gave me the $100 note.

I put more than $10 to God, put about $60 to the bank and put $30 to spend on a toy.

It took me long time to find the right thing, but I found it eventually, it was a cat I named Kitty-Kat. I took it home and put it on my bed.

Two years later we went to the beach for a holiday. I took Kitty-Kat with me. When we left I did not know that I had left Kitty-Kat behind. When I got home and unpacked I found Kitty-Kat was not there. We asked where we stayed but they said they hadn't seen it anywhere! I prayed and prayed even before school I prayed. One day we got a phone call. They said they had found Kitty-Kat in all of the sheets and pillows after they had all been washed. I said thankyou to God!! They said that I could have it when I went back to the place or in the post. I said that I wanted it in the post.

God cares about our lovable toys as well!

Healing power...

This was a few weeks ago at the beach again and I was walking on the rocks happily. Then I let out a scream. I had been bitten by a Jumping Jack ant. I fell down screaming. Mum took me down to the ocean [but she didn't know that I had been praying]. Then I said the pain had stopped and I told her that I had been praying. She said that it was amazing. But mum still insisted I put my feet in the water so that it would cool off. Mum took me back to the apartment and we got some ice on it. Then mum read to me Tumtum and Nutmeg number 1 [that she had bought at a book store and had thought I would like reading]. That afternoon I went for a BIG walk pain free!!!!!!!!!!!!

Post script: Did you know Jumping Jack ants are very poisonous and the pain levels from a bite can kill a baby? And a neighbour said that she had been bitten and she said that if a child got bitten they would have to be hospitalised there was so much pain. When she got bitten it was so bad that she could not walk for 3 days.

God keeps His promises...

Before this story I had been sick with a vomiting bug many times over 2009 and 2010. One time I vomited for ten days. The last time I had a vomiting bug for three days. This was last year. At that time God promised me that I would never be sick again... He kept His promise!!!

Well it was my mum's birthday. She was turning 40. We decided to go to a restaurant. On the way (in the car) I felt sick but did not vomit.

When we got there I still felt sick but I still did not vomit.

At the restaurant I did not want any food so I tried to read a book of **Magic Ballerina**, but that did not work. I sat on the couches there and mum prayed for me. Dad took me outside to get some fresh air. Then we went back home and it was the worst of all. I rushed to my room.

I lay down and prayed and the pain stopped. I told Dad.

Following the path...

On Sunday we where worshipping the Lord (at the front), when my mum saw her friend (J). We went over to her and started praying. (It was very powerful)!

When the worshipping stopped we went to the side of room. Another one of my mum's friend came with us. She got touched by God **so** much that my mum and a few others had to get her up and out of the room, I stayed there with J. While I was there I started running my fingers along the inside of her (J's) arm, (while the service was on).

After the service J came over to me and she said to me that while the service was on and while I was tickling her arm, I was following the path of the pain that she had (I did not know this at the time) and that while I was doing that the pain had left.

She also said that someone else had prayed for her and the pain in her heart had left.

Finding the lost plate...

I got an orthodontic plate in early August for my mouth. I thought that it would be fun to have one... but it wasn't! I found out that it hurt for three days and then it got really annoying to have in, because you had to take it in and out all the time, when I ate. I've got used to it now though.

A few weeks later, I came home from swimming after school and found that I could not find my plate :(

I thought I had taken it out for swimming but I did not know for not know for sure... I told mum and dad that I had lost it and that I did not know where it was. We looked in all sorts of places, the bench, the table, my room, the music room, we even scanned the floors and behind the pillows on the couches, in my plate box and we **even** looked in my mum's office, but there was no sign of it.

When we could not find it, we thought that we should try my school, because I thought that I may have taken it out at playtime and dropped it.

At dinner time, my mum taught me that I had a responsibility to take care of my plate and that it was a good lesson for me and that in the future I needed to be more careful because it was really expensive to replace and I would have to use up nearly a year's pocket money to pay for a replacement, if I was to pay for it.

So I've been taught a good lesson!

After dinner dad went out to find the plate in the school ground. I didn't go because it was too late and dark. So dad went out to my school with our (the family's) torch.

After dinner I was impatient to see if dad had found the plate... but he hadn't found it.

We had prayed all the time and hoped we would find it.

So, I was to go to the orthodontist the next day and I was very nervous.

The next day I went to school (as usual) and looked for my plate where I ate my lunch and snack... but it wasn't there. It was class time and I got to go and look for my plate out side but it still was not there!

After school my mum picked me up. I was **very** nervous and didn't want to go but mum had a surprise for me... and guess what it was... MY PLATE! What a surprise for me.

I was so relieved that I couldn't wait to tell every-one what had happened and most kids were amazed and so was I!

CONCLUSION

As I conclude this chapter I am aware of the hundreds of stories that could have been included, but for space. Don't forget that if you want to read many more you can go to www.godtestimonies. wordpress.com

May your heart be inspired and filled with faith by these testimonies. May the Spirit of the Lord arrest you with possibilities for your life with Him. I have prayed that you will have encountered Him - and received a renewed passion for Jesus and deep love for people. The possibilities arising from this journey are endless.

Chapter Nine

SUPPORTING
EMPHASES

The most offensive thing about the church is that it is dead.

– Rolland Baker –

Making disciples who view the normal Christian life as being like Jesus in every way is proving to be one of the most exciting adventures and privileges of my life. I have deliberately peppered the text of *Priorities* with some of our stories, most particularly in the previous chapter, to help you see the reality of this lifestyle for a group of Aussies who have been prepared to join in the adventure.

So far, I have devoted the core of *Priorities* to a focus on the main characteristics of what we have discovered in making disciples in the 21st century. However, there are any number of other issues that we emphasise continually that underpin and support these key characteristics. I'd like to make sure I have been as thorough as possible in outlining our discoveries and also want to conclude with three areas of supporting emphases:

- expectantly reading the bible;
- attributes of kingdom living; and
- acknowledging and overcoming hindrances to becoming like Jesus in every way.

These are 'the other things' we are doing to help our congregation take responsibility to become self-governing, innately powerful and inherently supernatural.

EXPECTANTLY READING THE BIBLE

The bible is the reference point for all disciple-making efforts. The bible stands alone as the primary source against which our own experiences and encounters must be tested. Our understanding of the normal Christian life finds its roots in the riveting and passionate stories and declarations of the Word of God. Yet for many Christians today, their love for the Word, as evidenced by the knowledge of it, is not all it could be.

To engage enthusiastically with the Word helps us as individuals to see that it describes who we are, what we can have, who He is and what He is like for us. It is a book of encounters and experiences around these topics. We can find ourselves in it because it is the living Word. With this framework it can empower people to live from heaven to earth.

The bible is not a book of memory verses, it is a book of experiences. There is a fundamental difference between bible knowing and bible believing. The bible from Genesis to Revelation is about people made in the image of God, who in the midst of their struggles, are discovering how to establish His kingdom on the earth. It is pulsating with the battle accounts of people who confidently stood their ground, knowing God always comes through.

The bible portrays the lives of people who desired to live out the life that God fully intended for them. They are intent on discovering the realities of heaven in the battleground of circumstances. They joined with God as His people to establish His inheritance on earth.

As we dive into the New Testament, we discover the place we have been given in Him. As He is, so are we in this world. We are to represent the fullness of God and the abundance of God. As Jesus was full of wisdom, power, blessing, glory, honour and might, so are we. It is the fullness of Him who fills all in all. We are in Christ, therefore we are subject to His fullness, majesty and inheritance. This is who we are on the earth.

It is not possible to be a bible believing Christian and maintain a theology of powerlessness. We have been made in His image so that we can choose His way of seeing, thinking, believing and walking. We can choose a brilliant way of life. A way of life that honours the truth – that we no longer live as aliens but as fellow citizens of heaven. As saints, we live knowing that circumstances cannot violate who we are in Christ. What we enter into in Christ is important, not what we are going through.

Jesus is astonishingly wonderful. I don't know how He has done it, but I am like Him. In Him we live and move and have our being. We have been granted His precious and magnificent promises so that we can be partakers of His divine nature. We are fellow heirs of Christ and partakers of His divine inheritance. We are in Christ to experience the fullness of who Jesus is.

What we enter into in Christ is important, not what we are going through. We are not to be earth bound in our thinking. We are to be ignited by our own revelatory experiences that are supported by the Word of God. Now, that's a book I want to live from!

ATTRIBUTES OF KINGDOM LIVING

Jesus came preaching the Kingdom of God. His call was to be reconciled to God (born again) so that we could see the Kingdom of God. Disciple making, as a rule, is expressed in church life. I think it is fair to speculate that our definitions and processes of disciple making have drifted so that we have disciples of *church* as much as if not more than we have disciples of the *kingdom*. In making disciples who are like Jesus in every way, it is important to develop their understanding of living in the Kingdom. So, here's a list of attributes of kingdom living I believe we can continue to build upon.

- Having hearts that burn with affection for God. This motivation results in:
  - a desire to host His presence with a result of being aware of co-labouring with Jesus to release the kingdom;
  - spiritual encounters, where we live for what we can experience, not what we know;
  - the knowledge that we cannot afford to have a thought in our heads that He does not have in His heart; and,
  - a realisation that we can put a demand on what the Lord has shown us.
- Approaching circumstances with a commitment to hold onto rest, peace, stillness, the knowledge of who we are in Christ and the power received through experiences and encounters.
- Learning to look at life's circumstances as a learner: learning who God is, how heaven thinks, who we are in Christ, how to access His resources and what His language is.
- Engaging with circumstances so that the fruit of the Spirit grows, not just to find answers. Looking to know and experience the nature and character of God.
- Living from the fruit of the Spirit keeps us in rest and peace, which in turn cuts down the place and posture of the enemy.
- Recognising that we are responsible for what we focus on, making it a priority to remember that Jesus has won absolute victory; I am significant; nothing is impossible and God is good.
- Receiving more of the kingdom and live conscious of what we already have.
- Responding to the Spirit and what already exists, allowing

heaven to set the agenda, not living in reaction to darkness nor being focussed on the demonic realm even though we live in conflict.

- Celebrating who someone is, rather than criticise what someone is not.

Moreover:

- God leads us **in** triumph because it is a process. God does not lead us **to** triumph because that is a destination. Process makes us rich not the outcome.
- When Jesus speaks to us it is to bring joy. (John 15:11)
- Choose a better thought. (2 Corinthians 4:16)
- Keep giving thanks, with a view to loosing consciousness of a difficult present to be in His presence.
- All trust needs to be joyful, otherwise it leads to anxiety.
- When walking into our future we often don't know how to get there so intimacy and fellowship with God are required.
- Don't feel how small you are; see how big God has made you.
- Growth in the Spirit is always relational.
- Our inheritance in Christ is not on the basis of performance it is on the basis of our placement in Christ.
- Grace takes us into a realm where we trust in His ability not ours.
- We are learning to partner with what we already have through grace.
- What worked with God in one season may not work in the next. There are apparent contradictory principles, such as 'receive the kingdom like little children' (inheritance) and 'take the kingdom by force' (warfare). A commitment to

being in God's presence helps us to discern as we learn to live from the voice of God.

- The more we yield and surrender to the presence of the Holy Spirit, the more He will entrust Himself to us.
- We are to release the Kingdom of God and its resources in to the earth through:
  - Our radical obedience;
  - Our faith;
  - Our declarations.
- We get into the kingdom by believing in God. The kingdom flourishes in us when we accept that God believes in us. Gideon's problem was in his 'stance' not in his circumstances. What Gideon need was already in him. He did not need anything new.
- What we tolerate, dominates.
- Every mystery is an invitation to encounter God. The lifestyle of the believer is to discover what God has hidden *for* us. (Proverbs 25:2) Hunger and desperation unlock the things God has hidden for us, not from us. This is why Jesus taught in parables because the receipt of revelation increases the responsibility of the one who receives. What we receive we have legal access to, but it comes with greater expectation – it is a matter of faithful stewardship.
- As we embrace risk we find strongholds in our thinking that need to be transformed.
- Jesus, the desire of all nations, has taken up residence in us to make us desirable.
- Whatever *reigns* in our lives will *rain* around us. The reality

in us becomes the reality around us. God wants to build our internal world so that the kingdom within us is greater than the kingdom around us.

- Peace in the kingdom of God is not the absence of conflict, anger or war; it is the presence of Jesus.
- Put my understanding on the shelf and move into trust.
- The earth is groaning for us to discover who we are and the authority we have.
- The heart of the matter is always a matter of the heart.

HINDRANCES

The adventure of living like Jesus in every way takes place in the context of a clash of two kingdoms. It is advantageous in warfare to know where the attacks come from and what they are aimed at. We also live in a culture that celebrates the exchange of ideas, which can result in us being robbed by human ideas because His ways are not our ways. Following are some hindrances that can be generated by spiritual attack on our own predisposition to process intellectually. Below each is a solution, or 'antidote' to help us overcome the obstacles they create for us. They are presented randomly and not as a prioritised list.

- Becoming satisfied with the glory we are seeing, with the result that a quest for more of/in God, plateaus and power stops flowing. Satisfaction leads to complacency.

  - *Antidote*: Embrace dissatisfaction as a motivation to keep pursuing, crying out and contending for miracles.

- Placing our attention on what God **isn't** doing, resulting in becoming bitter and resentful towards God while legitimising our unbelief. The pool of Bethesda recorded what Jesus did, not what He didn't do.

- *Antidote*: To celebrate what He is doing. Focussing on the glory that is being released so that we can go from glory to glory. Learning to discover what our kind, merciful and gracious Father has hidden *for* us not *from* us.

● When we place aspects of God's activity on the earth in the millennium we have released ourselves from the responsibility to pursue them.

- *Antidote*: Study to discover a 'Kingdom Now' theology.

● Instinctively look for a theology that makes us comfortable with what we already have, with the result that we are not stretched into discovering what is already ours.

- *Antidote*: Be like the Jews of Berea – Acts 17: 10–12

    The brethren immediately sent Paul and Silas away by night to Berea, and when they arrived, they went into the synagogue of the Jews. Now these were more noble-minded than those in Thessalonica, for they received the word with great eagerness, examining the Scriptures daily to see whether these things were so. Therefore many of them believed, along with a number of prominent Greek women and men.

● Faith being undermined by traditions, lack of breakthrough and our natural minds being offended by supernatural activity.

- *Antidote*: Faith comes by hearing **not** by having heard.

Abraham first heard 'sacrifice your son' but not long after he heard he went to look for the ram

- If we categorise the size of miracles, we lose our thankfulness and look for bigger and bigger miracles to feel awe for God.

  – *Antidote*: Delight in the person and presence of God, not the outcomes.

- Disappointment gives power to things we do not understand, robs us of things we do not understand and then begins to trade truth with lies.

  – *Antidote*: Be determined to offer a sacrifice of praise. It is only a sacrifice when we don't want or feel like joining in, but do so anyway.

- Regret torments the mind and chains the soul to the past. Imagine trying to drive a car forwards for 100 kilometres while constantly looking backwards!

  – *Antidote*: Discover the power of forgiveness. He has forgiven us so we need to learn how to forgive ourselves.

- A poverty spirit that focuses on meagre possibilities.

  – *Antidote*: Read the gospels and Jesus' approach to invading the impossible.

- When we lose sight of God as a Father who wants His family to invade the world with His kingdom, we lose sight of our true identity as sons of God.

  – *Antidote*: Submit to the empowerment of the Holy Spirit in order to believe in the work of the cross, to know we are in Christ to live a supernatural life and to see that we have a defeated enemy.

- ❧ When our attention is taken away from the presence of God, we are reduced from our place of authority and co-labouring with Jesus to a place of petition.

  – *Antidote*: Make personal adjustments to become more aware of the Holy Spirit in daily life.

EMBRACE THE ADVENTURE

The extraordinary reality for us at Stairway is that we have only just begun. So much more awaits us and those whom Jesus will teach and transform. To see our children so naturally embrace being like Jesus in every way is stunning. To cheer on our young people to carry the baton into a better future for the kingdom of God is exhilarating. To mobilise our mature congregation to be fathers and mothers to the next generations gives honour to who they are becoming and the price they have paid to get where we are. We encourage you to wholeheartedly pursue the adventure you were created for.

EPILOGUE

Even as we are readying this book for print, the stories of ordinary people living a supernatural lifestyle continue to flow to us. I am learning to walk a fine line. While I expect God to be Himself and turn up with healings, miracles, signs and wonders, I don't want to lose my amazement, gratitude and wonder that this extraordinary God we know and love wants to co-labour with us.

I couldn't let the opportunity pass to let you know about some of the more recent stories we have been told.

FROM MELBOURNE

No change in optic nerve but sight still restored...

On one of our recent healing nights at Stairway a man who was blind in one eye came along for prayer. Members of the prayer team believed with him for his sight and he received it. However, the miracle of his healing is that two days later he went to the doctor to have the healing confirmed. After the doctors had performed the appropriate tests they reported that he could indeed see but they couldn't explain why because the tests showed that his optic nerve was still dead!!

Operating table resurrection...

One of the men in our congregation works as a theatre orderly at a local hospital. He has a Christian friend who works as a theatre technician at the same hospital. The theatre technician had been part of a medical team that spent 45 minutes administering CPR to a woman whose heart had failed due to a congenital disorder. The medical team had pronounced her dead and were completing the paperwork to issue the death certificate.

At this point the theatre orderly from Stairway walked past the window of the theatre where this was taking place. The technician came out and suggested that both he and the orderly should pray for the lady to be raised from the dead. They prayed for a few minutes and as they stopped, which by this time was ten minutes since the patient had been pronounced dead, the heart monitor starting indicating that she was alive! The next day the orderly visited the lady and she was able to sit up in bed and hold a normal conversation.

A different kind of adjustment for the chiropractor...

Two Mondays ago I visited my chiropractor. He shared that his young toddler son was in ICU in hospital. On the previous Saturday night, his wife rushed to the kitchen after hearing their son's screams. She found him with suds and blood pouring from his mouth. He had managed to open the child safety lock on the kitchen cupboard and had inhaled and consumed dishwashing concentrate powder. He had sustained internal burns everywhere the powder had touched his tender flesh. Doctors felt he would survive but would later require operations to remove scar tissue as the burns healed. He would also likely suffer with future bouts of pneumonia and bronchial issues.

Our chiropractor does have a church background. His mum taught RE for years and is still a churchgoer, and of course was praying. I asked if I could pray for him and the situation, which I did there in his office. I asked if I could message our Stairway prayer group (which he knows about) to also pray. He was thankful for that to happen. I also sent him a text with a prayer he could use to pray over his son.

I messaged him on Wednesday to see how his son was progressing. His text in reply simply said: Your prayers worked. He's home and fine. I thought, 'Great. He's home ... but what about residual damage?' The following week I sent another message to check his progress. He responded with: Didn't you get my message last week? He's fine!

I saw the chiropractor again this week.

'How's Charlie?'

'He's great!'

He took out his phone and showed me Charlie's photo with a new haircut. Very cute and smiley! I asked what the doctors were saying now about him needing any follow up, as they had originally said he might. He said from the moment I prayed and sent the message out, Charlie was healed. There is absolutely nothing wrong with him. 'Isn't that what always happens when you ladies pray?'

FROM CAMBODIA

Stairway church has been involved in missionary endeavours in Cambodia for nearly twenty years. Recently members of our team were invited to train a group of pastors to 'hear and respond to the voice of God'. Here are some of the Cambodian pastors' testimonies as told to Steve Hyde, a good friend who has been living in Cambodia for the past eighteen years training and equipping indigenous Christian church leaders.

Seeking the true God...

Ta prayed to give thanks to the Lord and when he was prayed, the word of God came to Ta. The word was very precise. God said to Ta, 'I will lead you to a man who is seeking the true God. His name is "Lot"'. Ta knew that God would show him who the man was.

So, a few weeks ago he went to work in his field planting rice. He saw a man working in another rice field and God spoke to him, 'That's him.' Immediately, Ta left his planting and made his way over to the other man's field. He knew the man from around the village, but did not know him well, or even his name. As Ta approached, he had little small talk. He simply said, 'Lot, I know you are seeking the true God. I'll tell you about him.'

The man was shocked that Ta knew his name. Actually Cambodia is a country which rarely uses names; instead,in their culture, they refer to people by their age or title, out of respect. Most people speak to each other by simply using the words 'brother' or 'uncle' or 'grandmother'. Another reason that people do not use names is that they believe if you know a person's true name, you would be able to cast a spell on them or curse them using witchcraft. For most rural people, names are a heavily guarded secret. However, Ta was given the name of the man from God.

Lot, surprised that Ta knew his name, immediately stopped what he was doing. Ta continued by saying, 'You need to come and worship the true God, Jesus Christ, with me.' Immediately, Lot went with Ta to his home where Ta explained to him about Jesus Christ. Lot believed in Jesus and has been worshipping in the church since that day.

Diabetes gone...

Channy visited the town of Stong in Northwest Cambodia for the purpose of sharing the gospel. When she went there, the Lord gave her a word in her heart that she would meet a woman with diabetes who had no hope and Jesus would heal her. When Channy arrived in the town she went to the centre of town where she started sharing to people about Jesus. At a nearby house she saw a lady lying in front of her house.

In Cambodia, there is little medical assistance available for people. For basic fevers and colds there is medication, but for more serious ailments or injuries, there are few hospitals available to do more than basic medical treatment. Therefore, when people become sick with diseases like diabetes, there is no treatment for them. Basically, they just wait to die.

Channy approached the woman who was lying down. She noticed the women was very swollen and could hardly walk from the ravages of the disease. Channy shared with her that Jesus had given her a special word that she would be healed from diabetes so Channy proceeded to share with the lady about Jesus. However, quite honestly, Channy felt in her heart that she had no power, but Jesus spoke to her and said, 'I have the power to heal her'. So she prayed for the lady and immediately she was healed. The swelling vanished and the women could talk normally again and walk. She asked Channy if she could become a Christian and Channy has committed to return to the village regularly to teach her about following Jesus.

AIDS sufferer with no hope given new life...

Sopanny was working one day and heard the voice of God to go to the hospital, because there was a person who was dying and didn't have any hope. God specifically gave her the name "Vanny" who was dying of AIDS. Sophanny went to the only hospital in Poipet. She asked the first doctor she saw if anyone was dying there. The doctor told her there was a lady who is dying. Sophanny asked the name and the doctor told her the woman's name was, 'Vanny'. She knew that God wanted to heal Vanny.

So, she went to meet Vanny at her hospital bed and shared the gospel with her. Sophanny described Vanny's condition as horrible and hopeless. Vanny was in the final stages of AIDS. Her body had wasted away and sores covered her body, oozing with fluids. Anyone who saw Vanny was disgusted by her appearance. Vanny really looked pitiful. Sophanny laid her hands on Vanny and prayed for her. Vanny believed in Jesus at that point. As she prayed, Sophanny blessed Vanny.

The next day all the sores on Vanny were healed and she was in full strength. She has now returned to her previous work.

AN INVITATION

I trust you can see throughout the preceding pages that the congregation of Stairway Church has radically embraced a process of change. We have recognised that we couldn't just bolt on new beliefs to old behaviours. We needed to deconstruct our old theological persuasions and reconstruct a new theology based on what the Spirit is revealing today to His people.

The journey and process has been challenging yet incredibly rewarding, as you can see. We are growing as disciples of Jesus who are releasing the Kingdom of God. Jesus is being glorified, people are being touched by His love and we are excited to see the growth in our spirituality.

Wherever you are in the world and wherever you are attending church, the same journey is available for you to embark upon. The outcomes are stunning, and yet, above all else, the discovery of who God really is and who we are in Him is breathtaking. We are praying that you will be inspired to join in this history-making time of reformation.

NOTES

CHAPTER 1

1. facebook.com/note.php?note_id=191527057566092

CHAPTER 2

2. skipmoen.com. Search for "identity theft"